OXFORD
UNIVERSITY PRESS



fourth edition

# English File

## Intermediate Plus

Workbook

WITH KEY

Christina Latham-Koenig
Clive Oxenden
Kate Chomacki
with Jane Hudson

Paul Seligson and Clive Oxenden are the original co-authors of *English File 1* and *English File 2*

# Contents

# How to use your Workbook and Online Practice

## Student's Book

Use your Student's Book in class with your teacher.

**English File** fourth edition

| Workbook | | Online Practice |
|---|---|---|
| | ← | Look again at the Grammar, Vocabulary, and Pronunciation from the Student's Book before you do the Workbook exercises. |
| Practise ***Grammar***, ***Vocabulary***, and ***Pronunciation*** for every lesson. | → | Listen to the audio for the Pronunciation exercises. |
| | → | Use the Sound Bank videos to practise English sounds. |
| | ← | Watch the Practical English videos before you do the exercises. |
| Practise the ***Practical English*** for every episode. | → | Use the interactive video for more Practical English practice. |
| Do the ***Can you remember…?*** exercises to check that you remember the Grammar, Vocabulary, and Pronunciation every two Files. | → | Look again at the Grammar, Vocabulary and Pronunciation if you have any problems. |
| | | Practise Reading, Listening, Speaking and Writing. |

# 1A Why did they call you that?

*I call everyone 'Darling' because I can't remember their names.*
*Zsa Zsa Gabor, American actress*

**G** pronouns **V** names **P** vowel sounds

## 1 VOCABULARY names

**a** Match the sentence halves.

1

2

3

4

5

6

1 Her name's Katheryn, but she**'s called** __c__
2 Gordon Sumner's **nickname** ____
3 The singer **changed his name** from ____
4 Robert Downey Junior **is named after** ____
5 Ruth Rendell sometimes wrote under the **pseudonym** ____
6 Brad **is short** ____

a his father, Robert Downey Senior.
b Barbara Vine.
~~c Katy **for short**.~~
d **for** Bradley.
e is Sting.
f Peter Gene Hernandez to Bruno Mars.

**b** Complete the definitions with a word from the list.

~~first name~~ full name initials maiden name married name middle name

1 your _first name_ is a name that your parents choose for you when you are born
2 a ______________ is the name between a person's first name and surname
3 a woman's ______________ is her surname before she gets married
4 a woman's ______________ is her surname after she gets married
5 your ______________ is your whole name, including your first name, any middle names, and your family name
6 your ______________ are the first letters of all your names

**c** Complete the text with the words in **a** and **b**. Write one word in each space.

## The story behind a name

**Agatha Christie** is the bestselling novelist of all time. She wrote 66 detective stories under her own name and six romances under the [1] _pseudonym_ Mary Westmacott.

Agatha Christie's [2] __________ name and surname are known worldwide, but few people know what the rest of the writer's [3] __________, A.M.C.C., stand for. Agatha had two [4] __________ names, Mary and Clarissa, so her [5] __________ name was Agatha Mary Clarissa Christie. Christie was, in fact, her [6] __________ name – in 1914 she married Archie Christie ('Archie' is [7] __________ for Archibald). Agatha's [8] __________ name was Miller. Agatha and Archie Christie divorced in 1928, and when Agatha got married a second time – to the archaeologist Max Mallowan – she did not [9] __________ her name again.

As for Agatha Christie's family, she had a sister, Margaret Frary Miller, who was [10] __________ 'Madge' for short. Madge was [11] __________ after their grandmother's sister, Margaret West. Agatha also had a brother, Louis Montant Miller, whose [12] __________ was 'Monty'.

## VOCABULARY FROM SPEAKING

Complete the sentences with a word or phrase from the list.

a wide range of modern colours  brainpower
click together easily  delicious  ~~for creative people~~
good for the planet  healthy  recyclable
simple building system  warm light

1 Our art and design courses are suitable *for creative people* of all ages.
2 The ________________ from the lamp creates a relaxing atmosphere in the room.
3 The ________________ of some modern houses means they can be built in less than a day!
4 The soup's ________________. Can I have some more?
5 Do you think that doing crosswords improves your ________________?
6 The phone is available in ________________.
7 ________________ packaging is made of materials like glass or paper.
8 Our products are ________________ – they don't harm the environment.
9 If you want a ________________ snack, have some fruit.
10 The model plane is very simple to build because the parts ________________.

## 2 PRONUNCIATION vowel sounds

**a** Write the names in the chart.

~~Adele~~  Alex  Bill  Caroline  Chris  Emily
Eve  James  Joe  Kate  Leo  Mike  Paula
Sam  Sean  Sophie

|  1 cat |  2 train |  3 egg |  4 tree |
|---|---|---|---|
| | | *Adele* | |
|  5 fish |  6 bike |  7 horse |  8 phone |
| | | | |

**b** 1.1 Listen and check. Then listen again and repeat the names.

**c** 1.2 Listen and complete the sentences.

1 *Anna*'s carrying a *black bag*.

2 ________'s ________ a ________ today.

3 ________'s sending a ________ to a ________.

4 ________'s seeing his ________ this ________.

5 ________'s ________________ this year.

6 ________'s ________ is quite ________.

7 ________ is ordering ________________.

8 ________'s ________________ alone.

**d** 1.2 Listen again and repeat the sentences.

## 3 GRAMMAR pronouns

**a** Complete the sentences with a pronoun (*I*, *me*, *mine*, etc.) or a possessive adjective (*my*).

1 My wife and I are having a baby girl. We're going to call *her* Eloise.
2 I'd like you to meet my new boyfriend. ____________ name's Tom.
3 I'm staying at my sister's house. I always stay with ____________ when I go to the UK.
4 We aren't going to Emma and Ian's wedding. They haven't invited ____________.
5 Can I borrow your dictionary, please? I've forgotten ____________.
6 I have two nephews. ____________ names are Richard and Matthew.
7 We go everywhere by public transport. The bus stops right outside ____________ house.
8 Do you know where my keys are? I can't find ____________ anywhere.
9 My car is nearly out of petrol. Let's take ____________.
10 It's my dad's birthday tomorrow. I mustn't forget to call ____________.

**b** Circle the correct answer.

1 The children love that book. My husband reads *to them it* / *it to them*.
2 They gave *us their tickets* / *their tickets us*.
3 I'll send *a message you* / *you a message* when I arrive.
4 What do you think of my curtains? My mum made *them for me* / *for me them*.
5 She showed *me her holiday photos* / *her holiday photos me*.
6 I'm going to lend *a suitcase her* / *her a suitcase*.
7 Do you like my new phone? My cousin sold *to me it* / *it to me*.
8 Put on these gloves. I bought *them for you* / *for you them*.

**c** Complete the answers in the conversations. Change the word order and use pronouns and *to* / *for*.

1 A Who showed you the photo?
B Jack *showed it to me* ______.

2 A Who sent Sophie those flowers?
B Her husband ______.

3 A Who's going to buy your girlfriend a car?
B Her father ______.

4 A Who sold your parents their new car?
B Their neighbour ______.

5 A Who makes your lunch?
B My mum ______.

6 A Who gave you and your husband that picture?
B A colleague ______.

7 A Who's going to get you and your friends the tickets?
B My brother ______.

8 A Who's reading Max the story?
B His grandmother ______.

**d** Complete the text with the correct pronouns or possessive adjectives.

1 *My* ______ brother's first name is David – 2 ______'s called Dave for short. My parents gave 3 ______ that name because they liked 4 ______. His middle name is Robert. Robert was my grandfather's first name and my dad's middle name, so my brother is named after 5 ______. Dave's surname is the same as 6 ______: Hudson. 7 ______ nickname at school was Henry because 8 ______'s the first name of the famous explorer Henry Hudson.

**e** Write a short paragraph about your name. Include…

- your first name, what you're called for short, and why the name was chosen.
- your middle name, and why it was chosen.
- your surname.
- any nicknames and the reason for them.

______
______
______
______
______
______
______
______

**f** Write a similar paragraph about a family member or friend's name.

______
______
______
______
______
______
______
______



**Go online** for more practice

# Life in colour

Man needs colour to live. It's just as necessary an element as fire or water.
*Fernand Léger, French painter, sculptor, and film-maker*

**G** adjectives **V** adjective suffixes **P** word stress

## 1 VOCABULARY adjective suffixes

**a** Complete the sentences with the adjective form of the **bold** word. Use a suffix from the list.

*-able / -ible  -ate  -ive  -ous  -ful*

1 I think Charlie's very *attractive* – he always looks great! **ATTRACT**
2 My aunt is a very ________ woman. She volunteers at a hospital every weekend. **COMPASSION**
3 My girlfriend is very ________. She isn't afraid to express her opinion. **ASSERT**
4 It was very ________ of you to visit me in hospital. **THOUGHT**
5 Sue's a ________ child. We all adore her. **LOVE**
6 I'm very ________ of my friend's new car. **ENVY**
7 She's a ________ author. She's written many books and won several important prizes. **SUCCESS**
8 Jess is a ________ teenager. She often looks after the neighbour's children. **RESPONSE**
9 My sister is rather ________. She doesn't think before she acts. **IMPULSE**
10 My nephew is really ________. He often does my shopping for me. **HELP**
11 Philip was quite ________ in his teens, but now he's calmed down. **REBEL**
12 You have to be careful what you say to Helen. She's very ________. **SENSE**

**b** Complete the sentences. Make adjectives from the nouns and verbs from the list.

~~affection~~ consider create glamour possess power rely

1 Maria's children are very *affectionate*. They always give us a big hug when we arrive.
2 Matt's girlfriend is very ________. She doesn't let him talk to other girls.
3 My boss is quite ________. She always lets me take time off if my children are ill.
4 My assistant isn't very ________. I can't trust her to do anything important.
5 Lisa's very ________. She looks like an actress!
6 He's a very ________ businessman. He owns several large companies and he makes a lot of money.
7 Anna's really ________. She's made some wonderful sculptures.

**c** Complete the text with the adjective form of the words in brackets.

Last year, my friend Mark made a [1] *risky* (risk) investment: he bought an old house to repair and sell. Although it had once been one of the most expensive and [2] ________ (impress) buildings in the street, the house was [3] ________ (afford) because it was in such bad condition. The outside walls were [4] ________ (dirt) and damaged in places, which made the building quite [5] ________ (danger). The garden was [6] ________ (mess) because no one had looked after it for years. The windows didn't fit properly, so the house was cold and [7] ________ (noise) – you could hear the traffic outside.

Today the house is hardly [8] ________ (recognize). Downstairs, there's a [9] ________ living room with a sofa and some [10] ________ (comfort) armchairs. As well as an enormous kitchen, there's another room, which would be [11] ________ (suit) as a study or a small bedroom.

Upstairs, there's a [12] ________ (luxury) bathroom with a jacuzzi, as well as four tastefully-decorated bedrooms. Mark doesn't have a very [13] ________ (health) lifestyle, as he spends all day sitting at a desk, so he's installed a small gym in the attic.

The house is also much quieter and more [14] ________ (peace) now because the windows have been changed. The garden has been tidied, and it has some beautiful flowers, which makes it much more [15] ________ (colour). It's a very [16] ________ (rest) place to sit and have lunch or read a book.

Repairing a house can be quite [17] ________ (stress), but Mark is happy with the result. The repairs were [18] ________ (expense), but he's sure he has made a [19] ________ (profit) investment. The house is in a [20] ________ (desire) part of town, and he's calculated that it's now worth three times the money he paid for it.

**d** Make adjectives from the nouns and verbs in the list. Write them in the correct column.

~~care~~ colour end help hope peace power rest stress success thought use

| *-ful* and *-less* | only *-ful* | only *-less* |
|---|---|---|
| *careful / careless* | | |

## VOCABULARY FROM READING

Match colours 1–7 to definitions a–g.

| | | |
|---|---|---|
| 1 cream *c* | | a a dark reddish brown colour |
| 2 turquoise ___ | | b a dark brownish green colour |
| 3 navy ___ | | ~~c a pale yellowish white colour~~ |
| 4 scarlet ___ | | d a very dark blue colour |
| 5 khaki ___ | | e a bright red colour |
| 6 beige ___ | | f a light brown colour |
| 7 maroon ___ | | g a bright greenish-blue colour |

## 2 PRONUNCIATION word stress

**a** Underline the stressed syllable in the words from the list. Then write them in the correct column.

~~am|bi|tious~~ de|sir|a|ble en|vi|ous im|pul|sive in|ex|pen|sive ir|res|pon|si|ble pas|sion|ate re|be|lli|ous sen|si|ble so|cia|ble un|at|trac|tive un|suc|cess|ful

| Stress on first syllable | Stress on second syllable | Stress on third syllable |
|---|---|---|
| | *ambitious* | |

**b** 1.3 Listen and check. Then listen again and repeat the adjectives.

**c** Underline the stressed syllable in the words in each group. Then circle the word which has the stress on a different syllable.

1 as|ser|tive (col|our|ful) po|sse|ssive suc|cess|ful
2 at|trac|tive gla|mo|rous love|a|ble ris|ky
3 in|con|sid|er|ate re|spon|si|ble un|im|pre|ssive un|re|li|a|ble
4 af|ford|a|ble comfor|ta|ble prof|it|a|ble sui|ta|ble
5 af|fec|tion|ate cre|a|tive lu|xu|ri|ous po|wer|ful

**d** 1.4 Listen and check. Then listen again and repeat the adjectives.

## 3 GRAMMAR adjectives

**a** Correct the mistakes in the highlighted phrases.

1 She has a job stressful.
*a stressful job*
2 I love those purples flowers.
___
3 Sarah's more tall than her sister.
___
4 Silver isn't as expensive than gold.
___
5 My sister's the more reliable person I know.
___
6 He's the student more intelligent in our class.
___

**b** Complete the sentences with the correct comparative or superlative form of the adjective in brackets. More than one answer may be possible.

1 My car is *less powerful* than yours, but it's much more comfortable. (powerful)
2 I feel terrible! I'm ___ today than I was yesterday. (tired)
3 The road is ___ at the top of the hill than it is at the bottom, so you have to drive really carefully. (narrow)
4 Zach is one of ___ people I know – he's always upsetting people. (considerate)
5 The ___ person in my family is usually my mum – she's always worrying about something. (stressed)
6 The ___ solution would be to take a taxi so that we won't have to find somewhere to park. (simple)
7 The blue dress is ___ than the green one, so I'll buy the blue one. (expensive)

**c Complete the conversations with *one*, *ones*, or ✗ if neither word is necessary.**

1 A Do you prefer Chinese or Indian food?
B Indian ___✗___. I love really spicy food.

2 A Which biscuits shall I get?
B The chocolate *ones*________. They're my favourite.

3 A Which is your coat?
B The leather ___________.

4 A Where's your car?
B Over there. It's the green ___________.

5 A Shall I use brown or white bread for the sandwiches?
B Brown ___________. There isn't any white bread left.

6 A Which earrings do you like best?
B The gold ___________. They look great.

7 A Would you like still or sparkling mineral water?
B Sparkling ___________, please.

8 A Which trousers shall I get?
B The expensive ___________. They really suit you.

**d Complete the sentences with *much* or *a bit* + the comparative form of an adjective from the list.**

active ~~good~~ polite short spacious stressful thoughtful tidy

1 I'm feeling *a bit better* than yesterday, but I'm still not well enough to get out of bed.
2 I'm ________________ than my brother. He's 1.82 m and I'm 1.80 m.
3 My children are ________________ than my sister's. Hers never even say 'please' or 'thank you'.
4 His girlfriend is ________________ than he is. She always seems to know what he needs.
5 My new flat is ________________ than the old one. It's 80 $m^2$, and the old one was 50 $m^2$.
6 Cathy's ________________ than she used to be, but she still plays tennis, does Pilates, and goes jogging.
7 My husband's ________________ than me, but he doesn't put all his clothes away either.
8 Harry's new job is ________________ than his old one. Now he never works at weekends.

**e Complete the second sentence so that it means the same as the first sentence. Use the word in brackets. Write 3–5 words.**

1 Eddie isn't as ambitious as his brother. (less)
Eddie *is less ambitious than* his brother.
2 I've never heard an idea as stupid as that one. (the)
That's ________________ I've ever heard.
3 Those are the smartest trousers my uncle has. (ones)
Those trousers ________________ my uncle has.
4 Charlotte isn't quite as sensitive as she used to be. (bit)
Charlotte is ________________ she used to be.
5 The office at the end of the corridor is mine. (the)
My office is ________________ of the corridor.
6 My new car isn't as noisy as my old one. (quieter)
My new car ________________ my old one.
7 They weren't as bored yesterday as they are today. (than)
They ________________ they were yesterday.
8 The house on the corner is theirs. (the)
Their house is ________________.
9 Max isn't nearly as sociable as Tony. (much)
Tony ________________ Max.
10 I've never been as frightened as that in my life. (is)
That ________________ I've ever been in my life.

**f Use the words to write true sentences about you.**

1 much noisier than
________________________________
2 cleverer than
________________________________
3 my old one
________________________________
4 the least suitable
________________________________
5 a bit healthier than
________________________________
6 more affectionate than
________________________________
7 the most successful
________________________________
8 the messiest
________________________________

# Practical English A bad start

reporting lost luggage

## 1 REPORTING LOST LUGGAGE

Match sentences 1–10 to responses a–j.

1 Can I help you? *b*
2 Which flight were you on? ____
3 And you're a visitor to the UK? ____
4 How long are you staying for? ____
5 OK. How many bags are you missing? ____
6 Can you describe it for me? ____
7 And what size is it? ____
8 Anything else? ____
9 And what was in the bag? ____
10 Can I have your contact number in the UK? ____

a Clothes, toiletries, all my personal belongings.
~~b Yeah, my bag hasn't arrived.~~
c Yes, it has a logo.
d It's 07700 439826.
e Just one – a sports bag.
f Flight EZY6035 from Madrid.
g It's quite large.
h Well, it's dark blue…and it's made of canvas.
i Five days.
j Yes, that's right.

## 2 LANGUAGE FOCUS describing luggage

Complete the chart with the words from the list.

four wheels  greyish blue  hard plastic  a label  light green  medium size  ~~rucksack~~  small  suitcase  synthetic material

| Type of luggage | | |
|---|---|---|
| sports bag | *rucksack* | ____ |
| **Colour** | | |
| dark red | ____ | ____ |
| **Material** | | |
| canvas | ____ | ____ |
| **Size** | | |
| large | ____ | ____ |
| **Extras** | | |
| a logo | ____ | ____ |

## 3 SOCIAL ENGLISH

**a** Complete the highlighted phrases in the conversations with a word from the list.

awful  day  great  ~~lovely~~  miss  take  weird  wow

1 A It's *lovely* ____ to see you.
B It's ____ to see you, too.

2 A I can't believe we're here, Sophie.
B Neither can I. It's ____, isn't it?

3 A Look at this top I've just bought.
B Oh ____! It's amazing!

4 A I've lost my passport.
B It's not your ____, is it?

5 A I really ____ you.
B Me too.

6 A They've cancelled my flight.
B Oh no! That's ____.

7 A I'll put my bag in my room.
B Please, let me ____ that for you.

**b** Complete the conversations with the highlighted phrases from **a**.

1 A I can't believe you're so far away.
B Yes, *it's weird, isn't it?* It seems strange talking to you on the phone.
A ____
B Me, too.

2 A It's lovely to see you.
B ____
A I've brought you some flowers.
B ____ They're beautiful!

3 A I've been sitting in a traffic jam for two hours.
B Oh no! ____
A And now I'm finally here, I've just realized I've left my wallet at home.
B ____

4 A I'll put my bag in the boot.
B No, no, ____. It's too heavy for you.


**Go online** to practise the Practical English phrases

# Can you remember...? 1

## 1 GRAMMAR

Complete the sentences.

1 His name's Enrique, but he's called Kike f__________ sh__________.
2 This isn't my jacket. That beige one i__________ m__________.
3 This isn't my book. A friend lent it t__________ m__________.
4 I'm not looking for expensive trainers; I want to buy some ch__________ o__________.
5 It takes me a lot longer to get to work now because I live m__________ f__________ away than I used to.
6 My neighbours don't look after their garden. Theirs is th__________ l__________ attractive garden in the street.

## 2 VOCABULARY

Circle the word that is different.

1 maiden name married name first name surname
2 affection consider glamour compassion
3 affordable rebellious comfortable luxurious
4 envious thoughtless loveable possessive
5 stressful careful hopeful useful
6 pale messy bright dark

## 3 PRONUNCIATION

Circle the word with a different sound.

| | |
|---|---|
|  cat | 1 attractive careful glamorous married |
|  egg | 2 healthy messy possessive reliable |
|  horse | 3 affordable called colourful thoughtless |
|  train | 4 creative maiden compassionate spacious |
|  phone | 5 clothes hopeful profitable sociable |

## 4 GRAMMAR & VOCABULARY

Read the article. Circle a, b, or c.

### WHAT THE COLOUR OF YOUR CLOTHES SAYS ABOUT YOU

Some psychologists think that the colour of [1]____ clothes says a lot about us. They believe that red, purple, or grey clothes give people [2]____ impressions of what we are like.

Red clothes attract attention and suggest that the wearer is [3]____. Red is one of the [4]____ colours to wear when you want to impress or persuade someone to do something for [5]____. Black and blue are a bit [6]____ impressive than red, but they also suggest power. Black is more serious than the other two and suggests the wearer is confident and ambitious. If you are going to a job interview, you should probably wear blue, as it shows that you are [7]____ and can be trusted. People who are optimistic generally wear [8]____ brighter colours like pink, orange, or yellow. Purple indicates elegance, style, and [9]____ talent – it's a colour often worn by artists. Grey is the [10]____ neutral of all the colours. Grey clothes suggest that a person doesn't like attracting attention and would rather be on their own.

| | a | b | c |
|---|---|---|---|
| 1 | our | ours | their |
| 2 | difference | different | differents |
| 3 | careful | powerful | powerless |
| 4 | best | better | most |
| 5 | you | your | yours |
| 6 | least | less | the least |
| 7 | affordable | recognizable | reliable |
| 8 | bit | more | much |
| 9 | assertive | creative | sensitive |
| 10 | most | more | least |

Go online to check your progress

# 2A Get ready! Get set! Go!

> Holidays are about experiences and people, and tuning into what you feel like doing at the moment. Enjoy not having a watch.
> *Evelyn Glennie, British musician*

**G** present tenses **V** packing **P** /s/, /z/, and /ɪz/

## 1 VOCABULARY packing

**a** Circle the word that is different. Explain why.

1 bathrobe (sunhat) pyjamas slippers
The others are all *nightwear* .

2 toothpaste insect repellent adaptor make-up
The others are all ________________ .

3 pack of cards charger travel iron earphones
The others are all ________________ .

4 ID card visa driving licence razor
The others are all ________________ .

5 flip-flops swimsuit raincoat swimming trunks
The others are all ________________ .

**b** Complete the crossword.

ACROSS →

DOWN ↓

**c** Complete the text with the words and phrases from the lists.

**Nouns**

booking confirmation driving licence passport scissors shampoo travel insurance documents underwear visa washbag

**Verbs**

fold pack ~~roll up~~ unpack wrap

## TIPS FOR PACKING

**Next time you fly and you have to pack a small bag to take onto the plane and a suitcase for the hold, remember these tips.**

**First the suitcase:**

✔ Before you start, 1 *roll up* your jeans, jumpers, and T-shirts to make them smaller, and carefully 2 ________ your shirts and dresses.

✔ 3 ________ heavy items like shoes at the bottom of the case.

✔ Put a layer of jeans, jumpers, and T-shirts on top of the shoes.

✔ 4 ________ fragile items in a towel and put them in the middle of your case.

✔ Place shirts and dresses on top of the other clothes. You can 5 ________ them as soon as you arrive and hang them in a cupboard.

✔ Fill the spaces in your case with small items of clothing such as socks and 6 ________.

✔ Finally, put your 7 ________ with all your toiletries on the top. Remember that bottles of 8 ________ and deodorant over 100 ml must go in your case. Sharp objects like 9 ________ must also go in here.

**Now for your hand luggage:**

✔ Keep all your documents here. Make sure you have your 10 ________, in case the suitcase you have checked in gets lost.

✔ Take your 11 ________ to show you have paid for your accommodation.

✔ Have your 12 ________ with you in case you want to rent a car.

✔ Keep your ID card or 13 ________ in the outside pocket of the bag, if possible – you will probably need to show it more than once.

✔ Put your 14 ________ with your travel documents because you will need it to enter the country when you land.

**d** What would you need to pack for the following situations? Write five items.

1 a beach holiday in your own country

________

________

2 a three-day business trip abroad

________

________

## VOCABULARY FROM READING

Complete the sentences with a phrase from the list.

develop a magnetic pull get your revenge on ~~goes completely out the window~~ have the urge whatever the reason

1 My healthy eating routine always *goes completely out the window* when I go on holiday.
2 I often ________ to book a holiday in the sun when it's cold and wet outside.
3 One way to ________ an unfair employer is to start your own business.
4 ________, tourist numbers to the country have grown significantly in the last two years.
5 When I need to study, social media posts from people I don't even know ________.

## 2 PRONUNCIATION /s/, /z/, and /ɪz/

**a** 2.1 Listen and circle the word with a different sound.

| 1 snake | 2 zebra | 3 snake | 4 zebra | 5 snake |
|---|---|---|---|---|
| flip-flops<br>shoes<br>socks<br>sights | clothes<br>pyjamas<br>shorts<br>towels | visa<br>toothpaste<br>passport<br>sunscreen | razors<br>phones<br>cards<br>belts | books<br>scissors<br>laptops<br>jackets |

**b** 2.1 Listen again and repeat the words.

**c** Circle the word in each pair where the final *-es* is pronounced /ɪz/.

1 beaches clothes
2 gloves brushes
3 magazines sunglasses
4 cases headphones
5 bathrobes boxes
6 names addresses

**d** 2.2 Listen and check. Then listen again and repeat the words.

## 3 GRAMMAR present tenses

**a** Circle the correct form.

1 Be quiet! *I try* / *I'm trying* to read.
2 Ben *uses* / *is using* sunscreen all year round, not just in the summer.
3 Paul's wife *always packs* / *packs always* his suitcase for him.
4 Pay attention! You *don't listen* / *aren't listening* to me.
5 Elizabeth *doesn't usually wear* / *don't usually wear* make-up on the beach.
6 My boyfriend *always is* / *is always* late.
7 Sam and Richard *go* / *are going* hiking every weekend.
8 Who *your girlfriend is* / *is your girlfriend* talking to?
9 My brother *speaks* / *is speaking* good French because he has lived in France.
10 *You go* / *Do you go* to the same place on holiday every year?

**b** Complete the conversation with the present simple or present continuous form of the verbs in brackets.

A What [1] *are you doing* (do) next weekend?
B I [2] __________ (go) to a concert on Friday evening. Ed Sheeran [3] __________ (play) in Glasgow. I'm a real fan of his. [4] __________ you __________ (like) Ed Sheeran?
A I [5] __________ (not mind) him, but I wouldn't go all the way to Glasgow to see him. How [6] __________ you __________ (get) there?
B I [7] __________ (fly) on Friday morning. My flight [8] __________ (leave) at 14.25.
A What time [9] __________ the plane __________ (arrive) in Glasgow?
B We [10] __________ (land) at 15.15. My sister [11] __________ (pick me up) at the airport.
A What time is the concert?
B It [12] __________ (start) at 8.30. We [13] __________ (meet) some friends at 7.00 because we [14] __________ (not want) to be late.
A Well, I hope you have a great time.
B Thanks. I [15] __________ really __________ (look forward) to it!

**c** Complete the sentences with the present simple or present continuous form of a verb from the list.

not agree   not believe   belong   depend   have
not matter   recognize   see   think   not want

1 Susie's going to be late tonight. She*'s seeing* a friend after work.
2 I __________ that man. I've seen him before somewhere.
3 Josh isn't sure what to do this summer. He __________ about doing voluntary work.
4 Whose bag is this? __________ to you?
5 I __________ to buy anything. I'm just looking.
6 Can you call back later? We __________ dinner.
7 That isn't right. I __________ with you at all.
8 Sorry, I __________ in ghosts. I'm sure there's an explanation for what happened.
9 Don't worry about her comments. It __________ what other people say.
10 We might go camping, but it __________ on the weather.

**d** Use the words to write questions to ask someone about their next trip. Use the present simple or present continuous form of the verbs.

1 where / go
*Where are you going?*
2 who / go with
__________
3 where / stay
__________
4 how / get there
__________
5 what / want to do while you're there
__________
6 what / need to pack
__________
7 why / you / look forward to it
__________

**e** Answer the questions in **d** about your next trip.

1 __________
2 __________
3 __________
4 __________
5 __________
6 __________
7 __________


Go online for more practice

# 2B Go to checkout

If I won the lottery, I'd start a charity that helped little family hardware shops and fruit shops to open in city centres.
*Alexei Sayle, British comedian*

**G** possessives **V** shops and services **P** r and final -r

## 1 GRAMMAR possessives

**a Re-order the words to make sentences.**

1 my / house / we / day / the / at / spent / sister's
*We spent the day at my sister's house.*
2 go / Kate's / to / wedding / we / didn't
______________________
3 boyfriend's / with / doesn't / her / on / Beth / get / parents
______________________
4 house / of / the / is / door / locked / the / back
______________________
5 the / class / I / of / sit / always / the / front / at /
______________________

**b Circle the correct answer. Tick (✓) if both are correct.**

1 *The boy's bikes* / *The boys' bikes* need cleaning before they put them away. (circled: *The boys' bikes*)
2 That girl is *James' new girlfriend* / *James's new girlfriend*. ✓
3 It's *my mum's birthday* / *my mums' birthday* today.
4 There are a lot of *women's clothes* / *womens' clothes* in the charity shop.
5 She doesn't mind looking after *other people's* / *other peoples'* children.
6 There's a barbecue on Saturday at *John's* / *John's house*.
7 I'm going to *the hairdresser's* / *the hairdresser* after lunch.
8 That's *Poppy's and Mikey's school* / *Poppy and Mikey's school*.

**c Rewrite the highlighted phrase using *of* to show possession.**

1 Alice is one of my friends.
Alice is *a friend of mine*.
2 Eating too fast is one of his bad habits.
Eating too fast is a ______________.
3 How's your brother?
How's that ______________?
4 That woman is one of Lucy's teachers.
That woman is a ______________?
5 What's their idea?
What's this ______________?

**d Complete the sentences. Use *own* with a possessive adjective (*my, your, her*, etc.).**

1 My parents make *their own* bread.
2 I'd love to have a room of __________.
3 Does the house have __________ swimming pool?
4 That's my pen. Why don't you use __________?
5 We're taking __________ tent when we go camping.
6 My sister has just left home and moved into a place of __________.
7 My grandfather is 91 and he still has all __________ teeth.

**e Answer the questions about you. Use *'s, of,* or *own*.**

1 Whose house do you live in?
______________________
2 Whose bedroom is the biggest in your house or flat?
______________________
3 Whose was the last car you drove?
______________________
4 Where do you usually sit on a bus?
______________________
5 Whose was the last house you went to, and when?
______________________
6 Whose advice do you often take?
______________________

## 2 PRONUNCIATION *r* and final *-r*

**a** Circle where *-r* is pronounced /r/.

1 car showroom
2 dry cleaner's
3 greengrocer's
4 hairdresser's
5 garden centre
6 charity shop

**b** 2.3 Listen and check. Then listen again and repeat the words.

**c** 2.4 Listen and write the sentences. Circle *-r* when it is pronounced /r/.

1 *We're out of sugar.*
2 ____________________
3 ____________________
4 ____________________
5 ____________________

**d** 2.4 Listen again and repeat the sentences.

## 3 VOCABULARY shops and services

**a** Read the clues. Complete the puzzle to find the hidden kind of shop. What does it sell?

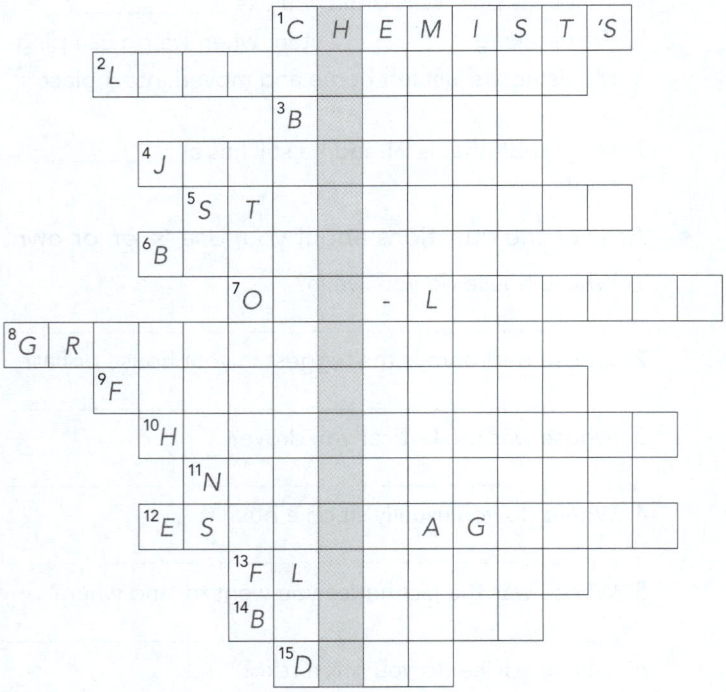


1 A shop that sells medicine and toiletries.
2 A type of shop where you pay to wash and dry your clothes in machines.
3 A shop that sells bread.
4 A shop where jewellery and watches are sold and repaired.
5 A shop that sells paper, pens, and pencils.
6 A shop that sells meat.
7 A shop that sells alcoholic drinks.
8 A shop that sells fruit and vegetables.
9 A shop that sells fish.
10 A shop where you can get your hair cut, washed, and styled.
11 A shop that sells newspapers and magazines.
12 A company that helps people buy, sell, or rent houses.
13 A shop that sells flowers.
14 A shop where men can have their hair cut.
15 A shop that sells cooked meats and cheeses.

**b** Join a word from **A** with a word from **B** to make places on the high street. Then complete the sentences.

**A** car chain charity craft DIY dry garden ~~market~~ pound travel

**B** agent's centre cleaner's fair shop (x2) showroom ~~stall~~ store (x2)

1 My cousin has a *market stall* selling leather bags in Covent Garden.
2 Can you pick up my suit from the ____________, please?
3 Tanya went to the ____________ to buy some plants.
4 Did you book your flights online or at the ____________?
5 We bought a beautiful hand-made wooden bowl at the ____________.
6 Zara is a ____________ that you find in many shopping centres all over the world.
7 We went to the ____________ to have a look at the new models.
8 Our local ____________ has a very good selection of gardening and carpentry tools.
9 The new ____________ has some lovely second-hand clothes.
10 Most things only cost 99p or less in the ____________.

**c** Replace the **bold** words in the sentences with the correct form of a phrasal verb from the list.

be out of  close down  ~~look for~~
look round  sell out  try on

1 Hannah was **trying to find** a bikini, but in the end she bought a swimsuit.
Hannah was *looking for* ________ a bikini, but in the end she bought a swimsuit.
2 I've **walked round to see what there is**, but I haven't seen anything I want to buy.
I've ________________, but I haven't seen anything I want to buy.
3 We'll have to go to the supermarket to get milk – the local shop **doesn't have any more to sell**.
We'll have to go to the supermarket to get milk – the local shop has ________________.
4 Excuse me, where can I **put on** these jeans **to see if they fit**?
Excuse me, where can I ________________ these jeans?
5 I didn't buy any black trousers because they **didn't have** my size **in stock**.
I didn't buy any black trousers because they ________________ my size.
6 The restaurant **stopped trading** after the health inspector's visit.
The restaurant ________________ after the health inspector's visit.

**d** Look at the photos. Where do you usually buy the items? Why?

1 *I usually buy flowers online because it's quicker.*
________________________________________
________________________________________
2 ________________________________________
________________________________________
3 ________________________________________
________________________________________
4 ________________________________________
________________________________________
5 ________________________________________
________________________________________
6 ________________________________________
________________________________________
7 ________________________________________
________________________________________
8 ________________________________________
________________________________________

## VOCABULARY FROM READING

Complete the sentences.

1 Our local supermarket st*ocks* ________ a wide range of organic products.
2 The fashion chain Zara has over a thousand br____________ across Europe.
3 Chain stores try to encourage l____________ c____________ by giving shoppers a store card.
4 My uncle's business is b____________ i____________ pr____________ after making a loss last year.
5 The company is making employees redundant in an attempt to c____________ c____________.

# 3A Grow up!

> Some people are old when they're 18 and some people are young when they're 90…
> *Yoko Ono, Japanese artist and songwriter*

**G** past simple, past continuous, or *used to?* **V** stages of life **P** *-ed* endings, sentence rhythm

## 1 VOCABULARY stages of life

**a** Look at the photos and complete the words.

1 a b*a b y*

2 a t__ __d__ __ __

3 a ch__ __ __

4 a pr__-t__ __ __

5 a t__ __n__g__ __

6 in her e__ __ __ __ tw__ __t__ __ __

7 in his m__ __-th__ __t__ __ __

8 in her l__ __ __ f__r__ __ __ __

9 r__ __ __r__ __

**b** Complete the sentences with the singular or plural form of the words and phrases in **a**.

1 Their *baby* is only two weeks old, so he spends most of his time sleeping.
2 One of the most important events for a ________-________ is starting secondary school.
3 I'm not sure how old Anna is. I'd say she's ________ ________ ________ ________, but I'm sure she isn't 50 yet.
4 ________ can be frustrating: they're often cheeky and they take little notice of their parents.
5 Paul is ________ ________ ________ ________; he'd like to settle down before he's 40.
6 ________ are exhausting: they've just learned to walk, and they have tantrums.
7 Laura has been at university for two or three years now, so she must be ________ ________ ________ ________.
8 My grandparents are in their late sixties and they're both ________.
9 Their son is so naughty that they've decided not to have any more ________.

**c** Write sentences about eight people in your family and the stages of life that they're in.

*My niece is a toddler.*

1 ________
2 ________
3 ________
4 ________
5 ________
6 ________
7 ________
8 ________

## 2 **GRAMMAR** past simple, past continuous, or *used to*?

**a** Circle the correct form.

1 I *didn't go out* / *wasn't going out* much when I was a teenager.
2 We *lived* / *used to live* in Germany for five years.
3 My brother *used to have* / *was having* a beard, but now he's shaved it off.
4 We *used to sit* / *were sitting* in the garden when my grandparents arrived.
5 Where *did you stay* / *were you staying* when you went on holiday to Greece?
6 I *didn't use to eat* / *wasn't eating* many vegetables when I was a child.
7 What *did you use to do* / *were you doing* when I saw you in town yesterday?
8 I gave up trying to explain when I realized that you *didn't listen* / *weren't listening*.
9 My girlfriend *became* / *used to become* a vegetarian when she was a student.
10 *Did you use to play* / *Were you playing* in the street when you were young?

**b** Complete the sentences with the correct form of the verbs in brackets. Use the past simple, past continuous, or *used to*. More than one answer may be possible.

1 Ben *didn't hear* the doorbell because he *was listening* to music with his headphones on. (not hear, listen)
2 I ________________ late this morning, so I ________________ time for breakfast. (wake up, not have)
3 When the phone rang, I ________________ to the children and my husband ________________ the dinner. (read, cook)
4 Emily ________________ glasses until she ________________ working at the computer all day. (not wear, start)
5 My parents ________________ a car until they ________________. (not have, get married)
6 Luckily, they ________________ very fast when they ________________ the lamp post. (not drive, hit)
7 I ________________ in Germany for a year when I ________________ a student. (live, be)
8 We ________________ in the high street, but then they ________________ a new hypermarket near our house. (go shopping, build)
9 My son ________________ his boarding pass while we ________________ at the airport for our flight. (lose, wait)
10 We always ________________ our holidays in the same village in France when we ________________ children. (spend, be)

**c** Complete the text with the correct form of the verbs in brackets. Use the past simple, past continuous, or *used to*. More than one answer may be possible.

I only ever [1] *met* (meet) one of my grandparents, and that was my dad's mother. We [2] ______ (see) her every Sunday afternoon when I was little. One day, my granny [3] ______ (look after) me while my parents [4] ______ (visit) a friend in hospital.

In the morning, I [5] ______ (play) in the garden, while my granny [6] ______ (cook) lunch. She [7] ______ (call) me when the meal was ready. Unfortunately, as I [8] ______ (run) into the kitchen I [9] ______ (catch) my little finger in the door and pulled off the nail. It [10] ______ (hurt) a lot, but I was more upset because I [11] ______ (not think) the nail would grow again. However, my granny patiently [12] ______ (explain) that I would soon have a new fingernail. After that, I [13] ______ (look forward to) seeing her every Sunday, so that I [14] ______ (can) show her how my nail [15] ______ (progress).

**d** Write true sentences about you at different stages of your life.

1 *When I was a baby, I used to cry a lot.*

2 ______

3 ______

4 ______

5 ______

6 ______

## 3 PRONUNCIATION *-ed* endings, sentence rhythm

**a** Write the past simple forms of these regular verbs in the chart according to the pronunciation of the *-ed* ending.

~~ask~~ change decide end hate hope live miss play start study travel want wash watch

|  1 **t**ie |  2 **d**og | /ɪd/ 3 |
|---|---|---|
| *asked* | | |

**b** 3.1 Listen and check. Then listen again and repeat the past simple forms.

**c** 3.2 Listen to six sentences. Write the verbs in the correct column. Use the context to help you.

| | Present | Past |
|---|---|---|
| 1 | | *walked* |
| 2 | | |
| 3 | | |
| 4 | | |
| 5 | | |
| 6 | | |

**d** 3.3 Listen and complete the sentences.

1 *Where* did you *play* when you were a *child*?

2 I ______ in the ______ near my ______.

3 I ______ to ______ when I was at ______.

4 This ______ when I was ______. I was with my ______, and we were ______ on the ______.

**e** 3.3 Listen again and repeat the sentences. Copy the rhythm.

 **Go online** for more practice

# Photo albums

When I say I want to photograph someone, what it really means is that I'd like to know them.
*Annie Leibovitz, American photographer*

**G** prepositions **V** photography **P** word stress

## 1 VOCABULARY photography

**a** Complete the description of the photo.

This photo was taken in a garden. In the [1]f*oreground*____, there's a woman and the trunk of a tree that has been cut down. The trunk is in the [2]b__________ right-hand corner of the photo, and the woman is standing [3]b__________ it. She's leaning on the tree trunk with her left hand on [4]t__________ of it. She's holding out her other hand. In the [5]c__________ of the photo is an older man. He looks much smaller than the woman because he's in the [6]d__________. It looks as if he's standing on the woman's hand. There's a bush in [7]fr__________ of the man, and [8]o__________ the woman there's a wall with a lot of flowers planted in it. In the [9]b__________, there are a lot of trees and in the top left-hand [10]c__________, there's a large white house.

**b** Complete the sentences with a word from the list.

close-up edit flash landscape lenses out of focus overexposed portrait setting ~~settings~~ zoomed in

1 My camera is automatic, so I don't have to change the *settings*____.
2 The photo's too dark because I forgot to use the __________.
3 I wanted to get a nice photo of my boyfriend, so I used the __________.
4 I sometimes __________ my photos before I share them on social media.
5 I __________ because the people were far away.
6 A professional photographer uses different __________ for scenic shots and close-ups.
7 You can't see the people clearly because the photo's very __________.
8 It can be difficult to get all of a __________ in a photo without using a wide-angle lens.
9 She was standing in direct sunlight, so the photo is __________.
10 This photo is a __________, so you can see all the details.

**c** Look at some recent photos on your phone. Use the words in **b** to describe six of them.

*There's a close-up of my sister.*
1 __________
2 __________
3 __________
4 __________
5 __________
6 __________

## VOCABULARY FROM READING

Complete the sentences with a word from the list.

~~back up~~ cancel go offline store upload

1 I'm going to *back up*____ my holiday photos because I don't want to lose them.
2 If you want to stop using social media, you have to __________ your accounts.
3 I __________ all my photos in separate albums on my laptop.
4 My husband has asked me not to __________ any photos of him to social media.
5 I want to watch a live concert on TV tonight, so I hope the streaming service doesn't __________.

## 2 PRONUNCIATION word stress

**a** Underline the stressed syllable in the words. Then put them in the correct column.

~~pho|to~~ pho|to|ge|nic pho|to|graph pho|to|gra|pher pho|to|gra|phic pho|to|gra|phy pho|to|shop

| Stress on first syllable | Stress on second syllable | Stress on third syllable |
|---|---|---|
| *photo* | | |

**b** 3.4 Listen and check. Then listen again and repeat the words.

**c** Underline the stressed syllable in the words from the list. Then circle the word which is stressed on the second syllable.

<u>back</u>|ground be|hind bo|ttom cor|ner fore|ground dis|tance

**d** 3.5 Listen and check. Then listen again and repeat the words.

## 3 GRAMMAR prepositions

**a** Match the sentence halves.

1 It was extremely hot inside *c*
2 There was a big garden in front of ____
3 We decided to have lunch outside in ____
4 We put some chairs on ____
5 We ate our lunch sitting under ____

a the house.
b the tree.
~~c our holiday cottage.~~
d the grass.
e the garden.

**b** Look at the pictures. Complete the sentences with the past simple of a verb from the list and the correct preposition.

climb ~~cycle~~ fall run sit down stand swim walk

across along down in front of next to ~~over~~ past up

1 We *cycled over* the bridge.
2 She ________________ the stairs.
3 The dog ________________ the river.
4 Mark ________________ Sophie.
5 They ________________ the pavement.
6 He ________________ a parked car.
7 The cat ________________ the tree
8 A tall man ________________ us.

**c** Circle the correct preposition.

1 We're very fond *about* / *of* / *to* our cat.
2 I'm very close *in* / *to* / *with* my sister.
3 I'm not very good *at* / *in* / *on* taking selfies.
4 She's angry *about* / *at* / *with* the photo I posted on her social media page.
5 Are you ready *at* / *for* / *in* a break?
6 He's disappointed *of* / *in* / *with* the camera on his new phone.
7 They aren't keen *in* / *of* / *on* photo exhibitions.
8 I'm very pleased *at* / *of* / *with* my profile photo.

**d** **Complete the second sentence so that it means the same as the first sentence. Use the word in brackets. Write 3–5 words.**

1 Whose is this camera? (belong)
Who *does this camera belong to*?
2 I can't wait to go on holiday. (looking forward)
I'm ______________________ on holiday.
3 The police officer said that everyone should go home. (told)
The police officer ______________________ home.
4 Mia managed to get a place at drama school. (succeed)
Mia ______________________ at drama school.
5 I think it's important to have a healthy diet. (believe)
I ______________________ a healthy diet.
6 He said sorry because he had forgotten my name. (apologized)
He ______________________ my name.
7 Everybody stopped talking when we went into the room. (entered)
When we ______________________, everyone stopped talking.
8 I didn't call my parents from the hotel because I got there too late. (arrived)
I ______________________ too late to call my parents.

**e** **Complete the sentences with a preposition where necessary.**

Do you know anyone who…
1 never smiles *at* ___________ the camera?
2 has photos of their friends ___________ the walls of their room?
3 is very proud ___________ a photo they've taken?
4 is worried ___________ sharing photos on social media?
5 prefers taking photos ___________ being in them?
6 has climbed ___________ a wall to take a photo?
7 has spent a lot of money ___________ a camera?
8 enjoys posing ___________ photos?
9 has married ___________ a photographer?
10 keeps family photos ___________ a purse or wallet?

**f** **Answer the questions in e about yourself and the people you know.**

1 *My son never smiles at the camera – he hates having his photo taken.*
______________________________________
2 ______________________________________
3 ______________________________________
4 ______________________________________
5 ______________________________________
6 ______________________________________
7 ______________________________________
8 ______________________________________
9 ______________________________________
10 ______________________________________

EPISODE 2

# Practical English All kinds of problems

renting a car

## 1 LANGUAGE FOCUS describing cars

**Complete the sentences with a word from the list.**

air conditioning automatic compact
convertible economy family ~~luxury~~
manual people carrier satnav

1 Audi and BMW are examples of *luxury* cars.
2 A __________ car usually has five doors.
3 You don't need to change gear in an __________.
4 Most cars today have __________, so you don't need to use a map to find your way.
5 An __________ car is usually the cheapest of the range.
6 On a sunny day, it's lots of fun driving a __________.
7 It gets very hot in the summer, so make sure your car has good __________.
8 If you don't mind changing gear, then get a __________ model.
9 You might need a __________ if you have a big family.
10 A __________ is great for driving in a city on your own.

## 2 RENTING A CAR

**Complete the missing words in the conversation.**

**A** Hi. Can I help you?
**B** Hello. Yes, I'd like to rent a car.
**A** Have you [1]h*ired* from us before?
**B** No, this is the first time.
**A** Could I see your [2]dr__________ l__________, please?
**B** Yes, here it is.
**A** What [3]k__________ of car are you looking for?
**B** I'd like a five-[4]d__________ family car. For a week.
**A** Automatic or [5]m__________?
**B** An automatic, please.
**A** Will there be any additional [6]dr__________?
**B** No, just me.
**A** OK, so we have several [7]m__________, but I'd recommend the Kia Nero. It's £95 per day, and that includes [8]in__________.
**B** That sounds good. Do I have to return it with a full petrol tank?
**A** Yes. If not, there's an extra [9]ch__________. You also have to pay any [10]p__________ tickets or speeding fines yourself.
**B** OK.
**A** Great! Let's go and look at the car.

## 3 SOCIAL ENGLISH

**a Complete the missing words in the phrases.**

1 Hi Emily. What's u*p*?
2 I'm a__________ I can't take your call at the moment.
3 Thanks Kieran. See you l__________.
4 Please leave your message after the t__________.
5 H__________ on. I'll get my coat.
6 I'm pr__________ tired.
7 Well, at l__________ we got home safely.

**b Complete the conversations with the highlighted phrases in a.**

**1 A** This is Caroline Phillips. *I'm afraid I can't take your call at the moment*. __________
**B** Hi Caroline. It's Karen. Just to tell you we're meeting at 8.30 tonight, not 8.00. __________

**2 A** Hi Oscar. __________
**B** I've had a terrible day.
**A** Well, __________ you're here now. Why don't you sit down, and I'll get you a drink.

**3 A** Do you want to go home now?
**B** Yes, it's really late, and __________
**A** OK, I'll get the bill.
**B** __________ Let me give you some money.
**A** No, don't worry. I'll get this.

**Go online** to practise the Practical English phrases

# Can you remember...? 1–3

## 1 GRAMMAR

Circle the correct words.

1 I didn't have time to queue for the concert tickets, so a friend got one *to me* / *for me*.
2 I hate spending money on sunglasses, so I always buy *the more* / *the least* expensive ones I can find.
3 I'm in my car. *I wait* / *I'm waiting* for my girlfriend outside her house.
4 Your children are old enough to make *their own* / *theirs own* lunch if you aren't at home.
5 Who did you *use to* / *used to* sit next to when you were at primary school?
6 We live near the airport, so a lot of planes *fly over* / *fly up* our house every day.

## 2 VOCABULARY

Circle the word that is different.

1 nail scissors slippers toothbrush comb
2 baker's butcher's fishmonger's stationer's
3 look round try on roll up look for
4 elderly old pre-teen retired
5 be cheeky be naughty get a mortgage have tantrums
6 flash settings lens overexposed

## 3 PRONUNCIATION

Circle the word with a different sound.

| | |
|---|---|
| fish | 1 slippers fishmonger visa initials |
| tree | 2 healthy teenager cleaners peaceful |
| right | 3 wrap background overexposed jeweller's |
| dog | 4 named rolled attracted relied |
| /ɪd/ | 5 edited zoomed folded collected |

## 4 GRAMMAR & VOCABULARY

Read the article. Circle a, b, or c.

### How to take good photos of children

In photography, one of the hardest shots to take is a [1]____ of a child. If you're taking photos [2]____ a room, you'll need a lot of light. Position the child near a window, but make sure the sun isn't shining [3]____ the window into the room. However, the [4]____ place to photograph children is outside. Wait until late afternoon or early evening when the sun is low in the sky. The most difficult children to capture are [5]____ – they've just learned to walk. The other problem is that children are usually [6]____ more interested in playing than in posing for a photo. You have to be [7]____ about getting their attention. You can use a noisy toy to get them to look [8]____ the camera, but don't show it [9]____ beforehand, or it won't be a surprise. Some [10]____ ask a friend to help distract the child while they try to get a picture. It isn't unusual to see an adult running round a room while another is taking photos of a child watching them.

| | | | |
|---|---|---|---|
| 1 | a flash | b landscape | c close-up |
| 2 | a inside | b into | c on |
| 3 | a across | b past | c through |
| 4 | a best | b better | c good |
| 5 | a babies | b teenagers | c toddlers |
| 6 | a bit | b much | c very |
| 7 | a considerate | b creative | c thoughtless |
| 8 | a after | b towards | c for |
| 9 | a at them | b for them | c to them |
| 10 | a photographers | b photography | c photographs |

**Go online** to check your progress

# 4A Don't throw it away!

> The thing about our garbage is that most of us never have to think about it again once we've thrown it in the trash.
> *Candida Brady, British director*

**G** future forms: *will / shall* and *be going to* **V** rubbish and recycling **P** /aɪ/ and /eɪ/

## 1 VOCABULARY rubbish and recycling

**a** Match the words from the list to definitions 1–5.

food waste ~~go to waste~~ supply supply chain surplus

1 not be used *go to waste*
2 an amount that is extra or more than you need ________
3 a system that creates products and delivers them to the customer ________
4 things you could eat that are thrown away ________
5 an amount of something that is available to be used ________

**b** Complete the text with the words from the list.

bins bin bags landfill site refuse collectors ~~rubbish~~ waste waste-paper basket

# What do you recycle?

In my family, we do our best to recycle as much of our [1] *rubbish* as possible. In the kitchen, we separate plastic, cans, and glass from other household [2] ________. The children each have a [3] ________ in their bedroom for used paper. When the [4] ________ are full, we take them outside and put them in different coloured [5] ________ on the street. The bin with all the material that can't be recycled is emptied every evening by the [6] ________. The contents are taken to a [7] ________. The green recycling bins with plastic, cans, paper, and glass, are emptied about once a week.

**c** Complete the words.

1 l *i d*

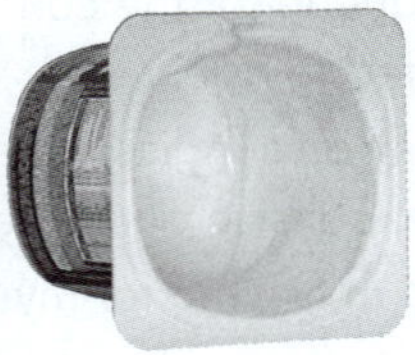

2 p__ __

3 t__ __

4 c__ __

5 j__ __

6 t__ __

7 p__ __ c__

8 c__ __ t__ __

9 b__ __ t__ __

10 p__ __ k__ __

11 wr__ __ p__ __

12 pl__ __ t__ __ b__ __

13 c__ __ __ b__ a__ __ b__ __

14 p__ __ __ s__ r__ __ __ tr__ __

15 s__ __ __ __ - b__ d__ __ __

**d** How are the following products usually sold? Write a word from **c**. More than one answer may be possible.

1 pasta sauce in a *pouch*
2 ice cream in a ______
3 jam in a ______
4 mineral water in a ______
5 crisps in a ______
6 sardines in a ______
7 soft drinks in a ______
8 yogurt in a ______

**e** Rewrite the **bold** phrases using a verb from the list.

reapply recycle ~~reheat~~ replay rethink reuse

1 Experts say that you should **warm up** food **again** only once. *reheat*
2 I have my own coffee cup that I can **use again** when I get a takeaway coffee. ______
3 This lipstick lasts for 24 hours, so you don't need to **put** it **on again** during the day. ______
4 Is it possible to **put** polystyrene trays **through a process so that they can be used again**? ______
5 The football match was abandoned because of bad weather, so they'll **play** it **again** on Wednesday. ______
6 Dan is going to have to **consider** his future **again** because he failed his final exams. ______

**f** Match the **bold** phrasal verbs in questions 1–4 to definitions a–d.

1 Who usually **takes out** the rubbish in your house? *c*
2 Have you ever **thrown away** something by mistake? ___
3 How often do the refuse collectors **take away** the rubbish in your area? ___
4 Do you **give away** your old clothes? Who to? ___

a to let somebody have something without wanting money in return
b to remove something and take it to another place
~~c to put something outside that was previously inside~~
d to get rid of rubbish or something that you don't want

**g** Answer the questions in **f** about you.

1 ______
2 ______
3 ______
4 ______

## VOCABULARY FROM READING

Match 1–6 to a–f to make compound nouns.

| | | |
|---|---|---|
| 1 baby | *c* | a bin |
| 2 pasta | ___ | b tray |
| 3 ready-meal | ___ | ~~c food~~ |
| 4 recycling | ___ | d sauce |
| 5 water | ___ | e paper |
| 6 wrapping | ___ | f bottle |

## 2 PRONUNCIATION /aɪ/ and /eɪ/

**a** Circle the word with a different sound.

| | |
|---|---|
| aɪ bike | 1 dec**i**de recyc**l**e s**i**te (tr**ay**) |
| eɪ train | 2 aw**ay** cont**ai**ner sell-b**y** w**a**ste |
| aɪ bike | 3 d**i**et d**a**te reappl**y** requ**i**re |
| eɪ train | 4 d**a**nger p**a**per repl**ay** suppl**y** |

**b** 4.1 Listen and check. Then listen again and repeat the words.

**c** Say the pairs of words. Do the **bold** letters have the same or different pronunciation? Write **S** (same) or **D** (different).

1 br**ea**k gr**ea**t *S*
2 **eye**s surv**ey** *D*
3 g**uy** w**i**-fi ___
4 h**eigh**t w**eigh**t ___
5 str**aigh**t fl**igh**t ___
6 b**uy** lifest**y**le ___

**d** 4.2 Listen and check. Then listen and repeat the words.

## 3 GRAMMAR future forms: *will / shall* and *be going to*

**a** Circle the correct future form. Tick (✓) if both forms are possible.

1. I'm so disappointed. *We're going to* / *We were going to* fly to Madrid tonight, but our flight has been cancelled.
2. *We're having* / *We're going to have* a barbecue next weekend. Do you want to come? ✓
3. It's too late to call them now. *They'll be* / *They're going to be* in bed.
4. *Shall I help* / *Will I help* you move the sofa?
5. Why don't you give away your riding boots? *You're never going to wear* / *You'll never wear* them again.
6. Trust me. *I won't tell* / *I'm not telling* anyone.
7. *I'm going to* / *I was going to* get up early, but I forgot to set my alarm.
8. My sister *is getting married* / *is going to get married* in the spring.
9. I'll be in London next weekend. *I'll stay* / *I'm going to stay* with my sister. We have all sorts of things planned.
10. Let's go for a walk now. I think *it's raining* / *it's going to rain* later.

**b** Complete the conversation with the correct forms of *will / shall* or *be going to*. More than one answer may be possible.

**A** Hi, Clare. Thanks for coming round to help.
**B** No problem. [1]*Are we going to pack* (we pack) everything up today?
**A** No, I'm moving next Saturday, so I have a whole week to sort things out.
**B** Right. So, what [2]__________ (we do) today?
**A** I thought we could start with the garage. Wait there and [3]__________ (I move) the car.
**B** Do you have any boxes?
**A** Yes, they're in the kitchen.
**B** OK, [4]__________ (I go) and get them for you.

* * *

**B** Right. Let's start. [5]__________ (you take) that ladder with you?
**A** No, I'm moving to a flat, so [6]__________ (I not have) room for it. [7]__________ (I give) it to one of my neighbours. [8]__________ (he come round) on Tuesday or Wednesday to pick it up.
**B** What about those old chairs? [9]__________ (you not have) room for those, either.
**A** Good point. What [10]__________ (I do) with them?
**B** Why don't you take them to the charity shop? Come on. [11]__________ (I help) you put them in the car.
**A** Be careful. They're heavy.
**B** Don't worry. [12]__________ (I not drop) them!

**c** Answer the questions about you. Use the correct future forms.

1. What are you going to do when you get home?
____________________
2. What do you think the weather will be like tomorrow?
____________________
3. What are you doing this weekend?
____________________
4. What are your plans for next summer?
____________________
____________________

 **Go online** for more practice

# 4B Put it on your CV

> I'm going to college. I don't care if it ruins my career. I'd rather be smart than a movie star.
> *Natalie Portman, American/Israeli actress*

**G** first and second conditionals **V** study and work **P** word stress

## 1 VOCABULARY study and work

**a** Complete the text with the words from the list.

~~academic and research staff~~ first degree further degree Master's degree PhD overseas students tutorials

### THE UNIVERSITY OF MANCHESTER

**Courses for over 40,000 students from 160 different countries**

The University of Manchester is one of the UK's largest universities. Around 6,000 [1] *academic and research staff* work there. It currently has over 40,000 students, both undergraduates studying for their [2] ________________ and graduates studying for a [3] ________________. These postgraduate qualifications might be a [4] ________________, normally a one-year course at the end of which a student has to write a dissertation, or a [5] ________________, a longer course during which students have to write a doctoral thesis. The university has nearly 11,000 [6] ________________ from 160 different countries. Students are taught through lectures, seminars, and [7] ________________.

**b** Complete the crossword.

**DOWN ↓**

1 A place where university students live.
2 A long piece of writing you do as part of a Master's degree.
3 The area of land where the main buildings of a university are.
5 A class in which a small group of students discuss a subject with a teacher.
6 A university teacher of the highest rank.
7 A university student who is studying for a further degree.
9 A teacher who is responsible for a small group of students at university.

**ACROSS →**

4 A seminar or other presentation given via the internet.
8 A talk that's given to a group of students to teach them about a particular subject.
10 A long piece of writing you do as part of a PhD.
11 A university student who is studying for their first degree.
12 One department in a university, e.g. for Arts or Law.

**c** Circle the correct words.

1 You need to apply for a *CV* / *work permit* if you get a job in another country.
2 You can apply for *a grant* / *an intern* to study at university if you can't afford to pay for the course.
3 You get a *job offer* / *job vacancy* if a company wants you to work for them.
4 You need to write a *covering letter* / *reference* to send with your CV.
5 You can apply for *experience* / *a scholarship* to study at university if your exam marks are very high.
6 If you're a student, you can get practical experience of a job by doing a six-week *apprenticeship* / *internship*.
7 You need to have academic *qualifications* / *skills* such as a PhD to become a researcher.
8 A company will invite you to *assist* / *attend* an interview if they think you might be suitable for a job.

**d** Complete the text with words from **c**.

When Maria finished university, she started looking out for [1]*job vacancies*____. With her degree in Business Administration, she found that she had the right [2]________ for some of the jobs, but she had no [3]________ because she had never worked before. One day, she saw an advert for a three-month [4]________ at a local company, so she decided to apply for it because she thought she might learn some useful [5]________. She carefully typed out her [6]________, including a record of her education and the jobs she had done, and asked her university tutor if he would give her a [7]________. After that, she wrote a [8]________ and emailed everything to the company. A week later, she received an email inviting her to [9]________ an interview. The day after, she was offered the position, but she decided not to accept it. She hadn't realized that if you work as an [10]________ you don't get paid anything!

## VOCABULARY FROM READING

Complete the sentences with a word from the list.

~~cash~~ checkout earned pocket money wages

1 How much *cash*________ do you have on you?
2 I didn't use to get much ________ when I was a child – only £1 a week.
3 I once ________ £200 in one day translating for a German company.
4 I can just about pay the rent out of my ________.
5 I didn't realize I'd lost my wallet until I went to pay for my shopping at the ________.

## 2 PRONUNCIATION word stress

**a** Underline the stressed syllable in the words from the list. Then write them in the correct column.

~~a|ttend~~ de|gree di|sser|ta|tion P|h|D post|gra|du|ate pro|fe|ssor re|fe|rence re|si|dence scho|lar|ship se|mi|nar tu|to|ri|al un|der|gra|du|ate va|can|cy

| Stress on first syllable | Stress on second syllable | Stress on third syllable |
|---|---|---|
| | *attend* | |

**b** 4.3 Listen and check. Then listen and repeat the words.

## 3 GRAMMAR first and second conditionals

**a** Match the sentence halves.

1 If I lost my job, *e*
2 If I stay in tonight, ___
3 If you can't attend a tutorial, ___
4 You won't get a good job ___
5 I won't go to the seminar ___
6 I'd be delighted ___
7 If I were you, ___
8 I wouldn't get a part-time job ___

a if I don't feel better tomorrow.
b you should let your tutor know.
c I'd get a room in a hall of residence.
d unless I needed the money.
e ~~I'd go abroad for a couple of years.~~
f if they offered me a place on the course.
g I can study for my exam.
h unless you get the right experience.

**b** Correct any mistakes in the highlighted phrases. Tick (✓) the correct sentences.

1 If I don't answer the phone, leave me a message. ✓
______
2 If he'll be late again, he might lose his job. ✗
*If he's late*
3 If they paid us more, we didn't complain.
______
4 You'd miss the traffic if you left a bit earlier.
______
5 We'll never finish everything if we won't work late.
______
6 If Sally lived in the city centre, she could walk to her office.
______
7 Max won't accept the job unless they don't agree to his conditions.
______
8 He does a postgraduate course if he can't find a job.
______
9 I wouldn't live at home if I'm a student.
______
10 If you didn't have a part-time job, you'd have more time to study.
______

**c** Write first and second conditional sentences.

1 My sister has a boyfriend, so she doesn't spend enough time studying.
My sister would spend more time studying if *she didn't have a boyfriend*.
2 I don't earn enough money, so I can't buy my own flat.
I could buy my own flat if ______.
3 Becky can only go to an American university if she gets a scholarship.
Becky ______ an American university unless she gets a scholarship.
4 Matt doesn't live in a hall of residence because it's too expensive.
If it wasn't so expensive, ______.
5 If I can't find a job, it's possible I'll do a Master's degree.
I ______ if I can't find a job.
6 I think you should wear a suit to the interview.
If ______, I'd wear a suit to the interview.
7 You miss your lectures because you get up late.
If you got up earlier, ______.
8 Students who don't attend lectures get into trouble.
If students don't attend lectures, ______.

**d** Complete the sentences about you.

1 If I can't do my homework, ______.
2 I'll go out tonight if ______.
3 I won't watch TV later unless ______.
4 If I hated my job, ______.
5 I'd be happier if ______.
6 I wouldn't move abroad unless ______.

# 5A Screen time

> If the use of leisure time is confined to looking at TV for a few extra hours every day, we will deteriorate as a people.
> *Eleanor Roosevelt, American former first lady*

**G** present perfect simple **V** television **P** /w/, /v/, and /b/

## 1 VOCABULARY television

**a** Complete the words with the missing vowels, *a*, *e*, *i*, *o*, or *u*.

1 cr*i*m*e* dr*a*m*a*

2 c__ __k__ry pr__gr__mm__

3 th__ w__ __th__r f__r__c__st

4 c__rr__nt __ff__ __rs pr__gr__mm__

5 c__rt__ __n

6 d__c__m__nt__ry

**b** Match the extracts to a type of programme from the list.

advert chat show live sport period drama ~~quiz show~~ reality show the news

1 'On tonight's show, two more contestants compete against each other to see who will go through to the next round.' *quiz show*
2 'If you don't sleep well, it can affect your whole day. Try taking SleepWell, the sleep aid guaranteed to give you a good night's rest.' ________
3 'Welcome to stage two of the most famous cycling race in the world.' ________
4 'So let's have a look at how the housemates have been getting on today...' ________
5 'Now on BBC1, a new dramatization of Charles Dickens's novel *Oliver Twist*.' ________
6 'Tonight Graham Norton talks to two special guests, actors Eddie Redmayne and Emma Stone.' ________
7 'And here, with the latest national and international stories on the hour, is Mark Finch.' ________

**c** Complete the sentences with a word from the list.

box set episode seasons series ~~sitcom~~ soap streaming service

1 *Friends* was an American *sitcom* about the romantic and often amusing adventures of a group of six friends living in New York.
2 More than 10 million viewers watched the final ________ of the TV drama, *Bodyguard*.
3 *Game of Thrones* is one of the most popular ________ ever shown on TV.
4 The British ________ *Coronation Street* follows the lives and problems of the neighbours on a fictional street.
5 The Harry Potter ________ contains all eight films.
6 The period drama *Downton Abbey* ran for a total of six ________.
7 Netflix is a ________ that distributes series like *Stranger Things* and *The Crown*.

**d** Match the **bold** phrasal verbs to definitions a–f.

1 Do you **turn on** the TV as soon as you get home? Why / Why not? *d*
2 What do you normally do first: fall asleep or **turn off** the TV? ____
3 How would you feel if someone **turned over** to another channel when you were watching something? ____
4 Which TV programme do you watch most often? When **is** it **on**? ____
5 When might you **turn** the TV **down**? ____
6 When would you **turn** it **up**? ____

a press a button to stop the TV working
b it's being shown on TV at this moment
c make the volume quieter
~~d press a button to start the TV working~~
e make the volume louder
f press a button to watch a different channel

**e** Answer the questions in **d** about you.

1 ________________
2 ________________
3 ________________
4 ________________
5 ________________
6 ________________

## VOCABULARY FROM LISTENING

Complete the sentences with a word from the list.

binge watched  catch-up  channels  ~~contestants~~  device  streaming  two-screen

1 The show starts with four pairs of *contestants*, but only one pair goes through to the final.
2 I know several people who ________ all five series of *Breaking Bad* in a week.
3 I missed my favourite soap last night, so I'm going to watch it on ________ tonight.
4 I usually tell people to put down their phones if they '________' while we're watching TV.
5 My family uses ________ services more than TV.
6 A huge number of TV ________ in the UK are available to watch online.
7 If you want to watch live TV online, you need a ________ like a tablet or a smartphone.

## 2 PRONUNCIATION /w/, /v/, and /b/

**a** 5.1 Listen and write the words you hear.

1 *vote* 5 ________
2 ________ 6 ________
3 ________ 7 ________
4 ________ 8 ________

**b** 5.1 Listen again and check. Then listen and repeat the words.

**c** 5.2 Listen and complete the sentences.

1 What's the *weather forecast* for the *weekend*?
2 The viewers ________ for the ________.
3 Have you ever ________ or Cambodia?
4 Did you ________ the ________ show on ________?
5 The ________ team won a ________.
6 We've been ________ since we set up our new ________.

**d** 5.2 Listen again and repeat the sentences.

## 3 GRAMMAR present perfect simple

**a** Correct any mistakes in the highlighted phrases. Tick (✓) the correct sentences.

1 Have you seen tomorrow's weather forecast? ✓
________________
2 The reporter haven't switched on her microphone. ✗
*hasn't switched on*
3 The documentary just has finished.
________________
4 They've had the same TV since 20 years.
________________
5 I've already seen this film.
________________
6 Have you ever be on TV?
________________
7 I haven't watched that programme since they changed the presenter.
________________
8 Lauren and Steve know each other for ages.
________________
9 I've never liked watching live sport.
________________
10 Hasn't yet the news started?
________________

**b Circle the correct words.**

1 Let's turn over. *We've seen / We saw* the news earlier.
2 There *has just been / just was* an earthquake in Thailand.
3 *I haven't wanted / I didn't want* to watch the film last night, so I went to bed.
4 Don't tell me what happens – *I haven't watched / I didn't watch* the last episode yet.
5 That programme *is on / has been on* since I was a child.
6 I don't need to see the film because *I've already read / I already read* the book.
7 The children have had the TV on *all day / for all day*.
8 They've only known each other *for a month / since a month* and they're getting married!

**c Complete the second sentence so that it has a similar meaning to the first sentence. Use the word in brackets.**

1 Jennifer Lawrence became an actress when she was a child. (since)
Jennifer Lawrence _has been an actress since_ she was a child.
2 My friend bought his speakers a week ago. (had)
My friend ______________________ a week.
3 I got home two minutes ago. (just)
I ______________________ home.
4 Is this your first time in Spain? (been)
______________________ before?
5 We moved house in 2005, 2008, and 2012. (times)
We ______________________.
6 I didn't like cartoons in the past, and I don't like them now. (never)
I ______________________ cartoons.
7 They've been married for ten years. (get)
They ______________________.
8 I don't want a coffee, thanks. I had one at home. (already)
I don't want a coffee, thanks. I ______________________.

**d Answer the questions. Write at least two sentences about each one.**

1 What's just happened in a TV series you're watching?
______________________________________________
______________________________________________
2 What's happened in the news today?
______________________________________________
______________________________________________
3 Which countries have you visited?
______________________________________________
______________________________________________
4 What new clothes have you bought recently?
______________________________________________
______________________________________________
5 What good things have happened recently in your family?
______________________________________________
______________________________________________


**Go online** for more practice

# 5B A quiet life?

> When I go out into the countryside and see the sun and the green and everything flowering, I say to myself 'Yes indeed, all that belongs to me!'
> *Henri Rousseau, French painter*

**G** present perfect continuous **V** the country **P** vowel sounds, sentence rhythm

## 1 VOCABULARY the country

**a** Order the letters to make words that match the definitions.

1 an area of land that is covered with trees (ODOW) *wood* ___________
2 a high area of land that is not as high as a mountain (LIHL) ___________
3 the low land between two mountains that often has a river flowing through it (LAYVEL) ___________
4 a small river (MASTER) ___________
5 a plant like a small, thick tree with many low branches (HUBS) ___________
6 the part of a fence that can be opened to let people through (TEGA) ___________
7 a large area of water that is surrounded by land (KEAL) ___________
8 an area of land in the country used for growing crops or keeping animals in (EDILF) ___________
9 a high, very steep area of rock, often next to the sea (FLICF) ___________
10 a deep hole in the ground where you can get water from (LEWL) ___________
11 small pieces of rock (TESOSN) ___________
12 a line of wooden posts to divide land or keep animals in (NECFE) ___________
13 a common green plant with thin leaves that covers fields and gardens (SGARS) ___________
14 a part of a tree that leaves, flowers, or fruit grow on (NBACRH) ___________
15 small thin pieces of wood from a tree (CKTISS) ___________
16 a row of bushes or small trees that separates one piece of land from another (DEGHE) ___________
17 soft, wet earth (DUM) ___________
18 large pieces of stone (SCKOR) ___________
19 a way across a piece of land that people can walk along (HAPT) ___________
20 one of the thin, flat, usually green parts of a plant or tree (FALE) ___________

**b** Complete the puzzle.

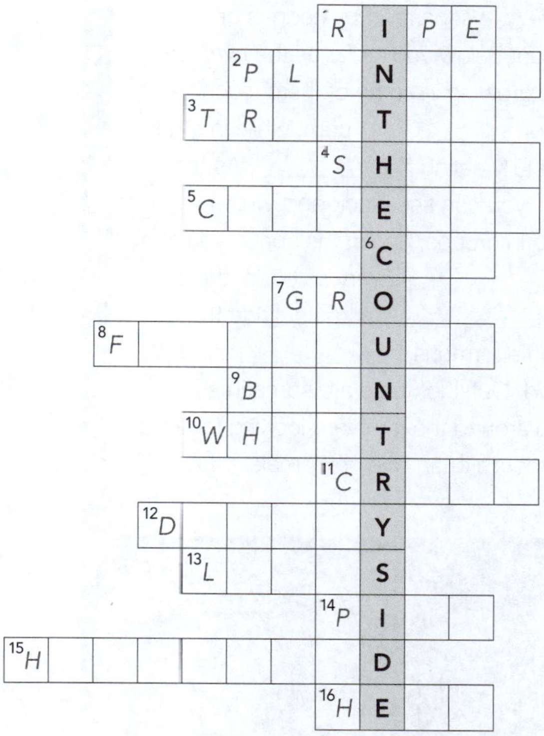


1 (used about fruit, etc.) ready to be picked and eaten
2 (of seeds) put in the ground to grow
3  4  5  6 
7 to put a plant in the ground and take care of it
8  9 
10 a cereal that can be made into flour
11 plants that are grown on farms for food
12  13 
14 to take a fruit or vegetable from the place where it is growing
15 (of fruit, crops, etc.) collected from the trees, fields, etc.
16 

**c** Complete the text with the words from the list.

barn cockerel cows crops fences ~~fields~~
grass hens lambs ripe tractor wheat

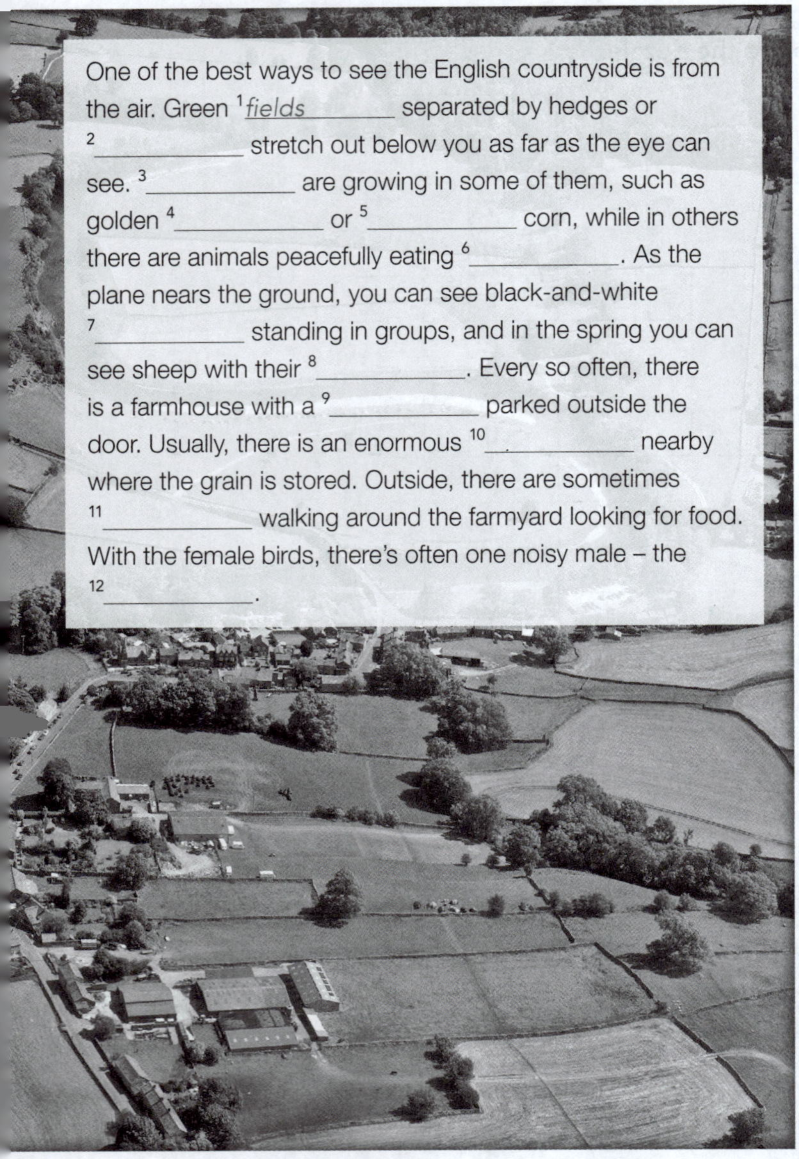

One of the best ways to see the English countryside is from the air. Green [1] *fields* ______ separated by hedges or [2] ________ stretch out below you as far as the eye can see. [3] ________ are growing in some of them, such as golden [4] ________ or [5] ________ corn, while in others there are animals peacefully eating [6] ________. As the plane nears the ground, you can see black-and-white [7] ________ standing in groups, and in the spring you can see sheep with their [8] ________. Every so often, there is a farmhouse with a [9] ________ parked outside the door. Usually, there is an enormous [10] ________ nearby where the grain is stored. Outside, there are sometimes [11] ________ walking around the farmyard looking for food. With the female birds, there's often one noisy male – the [12] ________.

**d** Write a short paragraph describing the countryside where you live. Use the text in **c** to help you.

________________________________________

________________________________________

________________________________________

________________________________________

________________________________________

________________________________________

________________________________________

________________________________________

________________________________________

________________________________________

## 2 PRONUNCIATION vowel sounds

**a** Circle the word with a different sound.

| | | |
|---|---|---|
| ɪ | fish | 1 cliff pick (ripe) sticks |
| iː | tree | 2 field hill leaf sheep |
| e | egg | 3 earth fence hedge threaten |
| æ | cat | 4 lambs harvest tractor valley |
| ɑː | car | 5 barn farm path warn |
| eɪ | train | 6 gate grass lake wait |
| ɒ | clock | 7 cockerel crops donkey stones |
| ʊ | bull | 8 bush look mud wood |
| aʊ | owl | 9 cow grow mountain town |

**b** 5.3 Listen and check. Then listen again and repeat the words.

**c** 5.4 Listen and complete the sentences.

1 I've been *riding* ____ my *bike* ____ to *work* ____ this week.
2 I've been ________ more ________ recently.
3 I've been ________ my ________.
4 I ________ been ________ so much ________.
5 I ________ been ________ that ________ lately.
6 I ________ been ________ much ________.

**d** 5.4 Listen again and repeat the sentences. Copy the rhythm.

## 3 GRAMMAR present perfect continuous

**a** **Complete the sentences with the present perfect continuous form of the verb in brackets. Use contractions if possible.**

1 I'm fed up with my friend. I*'ve been waiting* ______ for her for nearly an hour. (wait)
2 Charlie's bored. He ____________ history all day. (study)
3 I didn't know that you'd passed your test. How long ________ you ____________? (drive)
4 Tina's gone to the doctor's. She ____________ well recently. (not feel)
5 Mary and Paul aren't getting on. They ____________ a lot lately. (argue)
6 My parents are very excited about their holiday to Turkey. They ____________ it all year. (look forward to)
7 Your sister's really good at tennis. How long ________ she ____________? (play)
8 I think I've put on weight. I ____________ to the gym recently. (not go)

**b** **Complete the text with the present perfect continuous form of the verbs from the list. Use contractions if possible.**

not add drink not eat go make play swim ~~try~~ use walk

My husband and I [1] *have been trying* ______ to lead a healthier lifestyle recently. We [2] ____________ jogging together every day before we go to work. He [3] ____________ to work instead of driving, and I [4] ____________ the stairs at work instead of taking the lift. We [5] ____________ a lot of water during the day, and we [6] ____________ any snacks. After work, I [7] ____________ every evening and my husband [8] ____________ tennis twice a week. Instead of cooking a big meal when we get home, my husband [9] ____________ us some lovely salads. He [10] ____________ a lot of oil to the salads, but they still taste delicious!

**c** **Write present perfect continuous sentences with *for* or *since*. Use contractions if possible.**

1 I'm looking after my neighbours' dog. They went on holiday last Saturday.
*I've been looking after my neighbours' dog since last Saturday* ______.
2 My brother lives in Paris. He went there two years ago.
My brother ____________________.
3 Emma is my girlfriend. We started going out a year ago.
Emma and I ____________________.
4 Rosie is studying. She started when she came home.
Rosie ____________________.
5 They're training for the new season. Their first session was three weeks ago.
They ____________________.
6 It's raining. It started at about eight o'clock.
It ____________________.

**d** **What have you been doing recently? Write five sentences. Use the ideas from the list or your own ideas.**

at home at school / university / work with other people / alone exercise / food / hobbies / sleep

*I have exams, so I've been studying.*
*I've been eating more vegetables because I want to be healthier.*

1 ____________________
2 ____________________
3 ____________________
4 ____________________
5 ____________________

**Go online** for more practice | **Go online** to check your progress

EPISODE 3

# Practical English Time to tell the police

making a police report

## 1 MAKING A POLICE REPORT

**a** Re-order the words to make questions.

a do / know / you / her / were / what / plans / for / today
*Do you know what her plans were for today?*

b anything / notice / about / unusual / did / you / her
______

c your / aunt / missing / how / long / has / been
______

d you / were / where
______

e her / you / describe / can
______

f anything / tonight / there / about / the / unusual / was / house
______

g some / idea / her / normal / can / you / routine / of / give / me
______

h her / see / you / when / last / did
______

i she / was / remember / what / wearing / do / you
______

j anything / there / else / is
______

**b** Complete the conversation with the questions in **a**.

**A** Hello. I'd like to report a missing person – my aunt.
**B** OK, I'll take a statement. 1 *c*
**A** She was supposed to be home four hours ago.
**B** 2 ____
**A** Well, she's 55 years old. She's quite tall with long brown hair.
**B** 3 ____
**A** Around five o'clock last night.
**B** 4 ____
**A** At her house. I often go round on my way home from work.
**B** 5 ____
**A** A purple T-shirt and a pair of black leggings.
**B** 6 ____
**A** Well, I suppose she seemed a bit nervous.
**B** 7 ____
**A** No, she didn't mention anything.
**B** 8 ____
**A** She works from 8.00 to 4.00. She's always at home by 5.00.
**B** 9 ____
**A** Yes, the front door was unlocked, which was strange.
**B** 10 ____
**A** Yes, there is one other thing. Her handbag was on the table.

## 2 SOCIAL ENGLISH

**a** Complete the phrases with a word from the list.

carefully idea letting
mean message ~~right~~

1 I'm all *right* ______.
2 Thanks for ______ me stay.
3 Listen ______.
4 It's a ______ from
5 I have no ______.
6 What does it ______?

**b** Complete the conversations with the phrases in **a**.

1 **A** Where's everyone else?
**B** *I have no idea* ______.

2 **A** Can you tell me again what the homework is?
**B** Yes, but ______ this time! I won't repeat it again.

3 **A** I texted John and this is his reply.
**B** I don't understand. ______

4 **A** Are you sure you're OK?
**B** Yes, ______ Don't worry about me.

5 **A** Was that your phone?
**B** Yes. ______ my boyfriend.

6 **A** It was great to see you. Have you had a good time?
**B** Yes, I really like Budapest.
______

Go online to practise the Practical English phrases

# Can you remember...? 1–5

## 1 GRAMMAR

Complete the sentences.

1 My cousin Sue is m________ o________ th________ me. She's 56, and I'm only 32.
2 John is a good fr________ o________ m________. We've known each other for years.
3 I saw you sitting in your car last night. What w________ y________ d________?
4 I'm hungry. Where sh________ w________ g________ for lunch?
5 If we had a bigger house, I c________ h________ my own office.
6 I think we need to stop the car and have a break. We've b________ dr________ f________ nearly three hours.

## 2 VOCABULARY

Circle the word that is different.

1 fold unpack zoom in wrap
2 healthy messy noisy dirty
3 bin carton jar tub
4 seminar dissertation tutorial lecture
5 advert dissertation documentary series
6 lake stream gate well

## 3 PRONUNCIATION

Circle the word with a different sound.

| | |
|---|---|
|  train | 1 r**ai**ncoat h**eigh**t bak**e**r's w**eigh**t |
|  bike | 2 rec**y**cle beh**i**nd repl**ay** polyst**y**rene |
|  cat | 3 tr**a**ctor wr**a**pper b**a**tteries v**a**cancy |
|  car | 4 c**a**mpus dr**a**ma b**ar**n pyj**a**mas |
|  bull | 5 b**u**tcher's w**oo**d b**u**sh cart**oo**n |

## 4 GRAMMAR & VOCABULARY

Read the article. Circle a, b, or c.

# A British Institution

Every evening, people all over Britain tune in to BBC Radio 4 and listen to an introductory tune that [1]____ every night for more than 60 years. It is the theme tune to *The Archers*, the longest-running radio [2]____ in the world. *The Archers* is [3]____ just before seven o'clock. The programme is about life in the fictional village of Ambridge. The aim of the show was to give [4]____ information about new farming methods after the Second World War. The programme was originally about the lives of three farmers: Dan Archer, Walter Gabriel, and George Fairbrother, but a lot has changed [5]____ the first episode. The Archers' family farm, Brookfield, no longer belongs [6]____ Dan. First, it passed to Dan's son, Phil, and his wife Jill, and now it is owned by [7]____ four children. Their son, David, manages Brookfield, and he keeps animals as well as growing [8]____. The programme has been very [9]____, and at the height of its popularity, it was estimated that 60% of British adults were regular listeners. Today, it isn't quite as popular [10]____ it used to be, but it still has over a million listeners.

| | | | |
|---|---|---|---|
| 1 | a 's playing | b plays | c 's been playing |
| 2 | a chat show | b documentary | c soap |
| 3 | a in | b on | c up |
| 4 | a for farmers | b farmers | c to farmers |
| 5 | a since | b for | c from |
| 6 | a at | b of | c to |
| 7 | a Phil's and Jills' | b Phil and Jills' | c Phil and Jill's |
| 8 | a crops | b grass | c plants |
| 9 | a colourful | b successful | c useful |
| 10 | a as | b than | c that |

**Go online** to check your progress

# 6A What the waiter really thinks

Make the customer the hero of your story.
*Ann Handley, American marketer and author*

**G** obligation, necessity, prohibition, advice **V** at a restaurant **P** word pairs with *and*

## 1 VOCABULARY at a restaurant

**a** Complete the words.

1 m *u g*

2 o__ __ and v__ n __ g __ __

3 c __ __ d __ __

4 c __ __

5 s __ __ v __ __ g d __ __ h

6 f __ r __

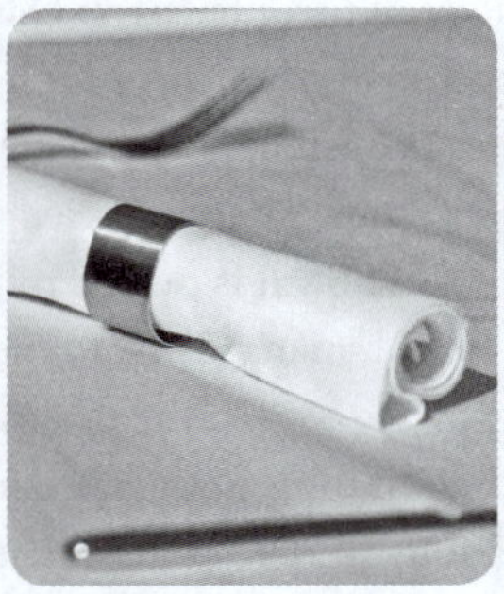

7 n __ __ k __ __

8 s __ __ t and p __ __ p __ __

9 t __ __ s __ __ __ n

10 g __ __ __ s

**b** Complete the sentences.

1 I'm hungry! I'm looking forward to a big pl*ate* of pasta.
2 He always has a b__________ of cereal for breakfast.
3 I'm looking for a c__________ to open the wine.
4 Let's ask for a j__________ of tap water instead of mineral water.
5 I'll lay the table for you. Which t__________ shall I use – the white one or the blue one?
6 Do you ever make tea in a t__________ or do you always make it in a mug?
7 Can I have another w__________ gl__________, please? I'm changing from white to red.
8 This kn__________ doesn't cut very well. Could you bring me another one?
9 I'm having the soup to start. Could I have a sp__________?
10 I don't like drinking tea out of a mug. I prefer using a cup and s__________.
11 I don't think I can carry all these drinks. Can I have a tr__________?

**c** Circle a, b, or c.

1 Can you make a list of what ____ I need to buy when I go shopping?
**a** dish **b** food **c** meal

2 Take a ____ and help yourself to some sandwiches.
**a** course **b** meal **c** plate

3 Bouillabaisse is a French ____ made with fish and seafood.
**a** course **b** dish **c** food

4 Some friends have invited us round for a ____ tonight.
**a** dish **b** meal **c** plate

5 I had soup for a starter and roast lamb for my main ____.
**a** course **b** food **c** plate

**d** Complete the text with the verbs from the list.

asked for booked carried cleared left poured ordered ~~recommended~~ sent back served took tried

Some friends [1] *recommended* a dish for us to try while we were on holiday: lobster stew. The restaurant our friends usually go to was full, so we [2] ______ a table at a different restaurant. When we arrived, the waiter showed us to our table, but it hadn't been cleaned. He [3] ______ the table for us and [4] ______ our drinks order. Then he disappeared for ages. He [5] ______ all the other customers before he brought us our drinks. He [6] ______ the wine, and we [7] ______ our food. When we [8] ______ the wine, it tasted like vinegar, so we [9] ______ it ______ and ordered some water instead. Eventually our food arrived. The waiter [10] ______ the tray with the lobster stew to our table, but he fell before he reached us. The boiling hot stew went all over my son's chair – luckily, he was in the toilets at the time. We [11] ______ the bill, [12] ______ no tip, and almost ran out of the restaurant.

**e** Answer the questions about you.

What do you put on the table when…?

1 you're eating alone

______

______

2 you're having lunch with your family

______

______

3 you invite a guest to dinner

______

______

## VOCABULARY FROM READING

Complete the sentences with a word from the list.

overcooked overworked ~~undercooked~~ understaffed

1 I sent my chicken back because it was *undercooked*. It was still pink in the middle.
2 The waiter was really ______ that night because three other members of staff were ill.
3 My vegetables were ______. They were soft, and they didn't taste of anything.
4 There aren't enough waiters in that restaurant. They're ______.

## 2 PRONUNCIATION word pairs with *and*

**a** Match the words to make word pairs.

| | | |
|---|---|---|
| 1 bacon | *b* | a and fork |
| 2 ice | ___ | ~~b and eggs~~ |
| 3 knife | ___ | c and cream |
| 4 milk | ___ | d and lemon |
| 5 strawberries | ___ | e and biscuits |
| 6 tea | ___ | f and sugar |

**b** 6.1 Listen and check. Then listen again and repeat the phrases.

**c** 6.2 Listen and complete the sentences.

1 Can you pass the *salt and pepper*, please?
2 Let's have ______ for lunch.
3 Would you like some ______ with your meal?
4 Have you put ______ on the salad?
5 Would you like a mug or a ______ for your tea?

**d** 6.2 Listen again and repeat the sentences.

## 3 GRAMMAR obligation, necessity, prohibition, advice

**a** Match the highlighted phrases in 1–7 to their meaning in a–g.

1 You don't have to get a visa if you're an EU citizen. *b*
2 You have to pay for your drinks when the waiter brings them to your table. ___
3 You ought to go to the doctor's if you aren't feeling well. ___
4 You shouldn't have a big meal late at night. ___
5 You needn't take an umbrella. It isn't raining. ___
6 You mustn't leave the path when you're walking around the island. ___
7 This is a great book – you must read it. ___

a You're obliged to do it.
~~b There's no obligation for you to do it.~~
c It's important to me that you do it.
d It's prohibited.
e It isn't necessary for you to do it.
f It's the right thing to do.
g It isn't the right thing to do.

**b** Circle the correct verbs. In each sentence two are correct and one is wrong.

1 I think we __________ tell them about the mistake on the bill. They've forgotten the drinks.
  **a** must **b** ought to **c** should
2 The speed limit on this road is 30 kph, so you __________ drive faster than that.
  **a** shouldn't **b** don't have to **c** mustn't
3 Service is included in the bill. We __________ leave a tip.
  **a** don't have to **b** needn't **c** mustn't
4 I __________ call my mum tonight – it's her birthday.
  **a** have to **b** must **c** needn't
5 You __________ speak badly about other people. It isn't very nice.
  **a** don't have to **b** oughtn't to **c** shouldn't
6 You __________ try the seafood while you're in Sicily – it's delicious.
  **a** have to **b** must **c** need
7 My neighbour __________ take her son to the doctor's last night.
  **a** had to **b** must **c** needed to

**c** Complete the second sentence so it means the same as the first sentence. More than one answer may be possible.

1 It isn't a good idea to keep takeaway food for a long time.
  You *shouldn't keep takeaway food* for a long time.
2 In some countries, it's prohibited to make a noise after 10.00 p.m.
  In some countries, you __________ after 10.00 p.m.
3 Builders are obliged to wear a helmet on a building site.
  Builders __________ on a building site.
4 It isn't necessary for you to iron your shirt this morning because I did it last night!
  You __________ your shirt this morning because I did it last night!
5 If you go to that restaurant, it's a good idea to order the steak.
  You __________ if you go to that restaurant.
6 We aren't obliged to pay any bills because everything is included in the rent.
  We __________ any bills because everything is included in the rent.
7 In my country, people are obliged to take old batteries to a recycling point.
  In my country, you __________ to a recycling point.
8 It's dangerous to let children play with matches.
  You __________ with matches.

**d** Think about good waiters and waitresses. Write five sentences using the modal verbs in **A**. Use the ideas in **B** or your own ideas.

**A** have to must need to ought to should

**B** appearance customer service mistakes personality skills

*They should be friendly.*

1 __________
2 __________
3 __________
4 __________
5 __________


Go online for more practice

# 6B Do it yourself

> If you want a thing done well, do it yourself.
> *Napoleon Bonaparte, 19th century Emperor of the French*

**G** *can, could,* and *be able to* **V** DIY and repairs, paraphrasing **P** consonant clusters

## 1 GRAMMAR *can, could,* and *be able to*

**a** Circle the correct form. Tick (✓) if both are correct.

1. My mother *could / was able to* sew really well when she was younger. ✓
2. You need to *can / be able to* forget your personal problems when you're at work.
3. Everyone in the office *is able to / can* use the new software program.
4. If it's nice this evening, *we can / we'll be able to* have a barbecue.
5. £30 for a salad and a mineral water? That *can't / isn't able to* be right!
6. If your brother's restaurant was nearer, we *could / would be able to* go more often.
7. To work for this company, you must *can / be able to* speak three languages.
8. We're really sorry we *couldn't / weren't able to* come to your party.
9. I've never *could / been able to* dance very well, but I'd love to learn.
10. *Can you / Will you be able to* pick me up at the airport?
11. They wouldn't give me a refund for the top, but I *could / was able to* change it for a new one.
12. I hate *not can / not being able to* read a menu when I'm abroad.

**b** Rewrite the highlighted sentences using the correct form of *can* or *be able to*. If both forms are possible, write two sentences.

1. Is it OK if I close the window? I'm really cold.
   *Can I close the window?*
2. It isn't possible for me to come to the party. I'll be on holiday.
   *I can't come to the party. / I won't be able to come to the party.*
3. Is it OK if I sit here? It's the only free seat.
   ______
4. It hasn't been possible for me to reply sooner. I've been very busy.
   ______
5. It wasn't possible for her to finish the meal. There was too much food.
   ______
6. They're staying in a self-catering apartment. They want to have the possibility of cooking their own meals.
   ______
7. I'm sure that isn't John. He's on holiday.
   ______
8. We're delighted that it is possible for us to come to dinner. We're looking forward to it.
   ______
9. I love having the possibility of getting up late in the holidays. I usually start work at eight o'clock.
   ______
10. We managed to book a room with a sea view. It was the last one available.
   ______

**c** Answer the questions about you.

1. What could you do really well as a child?
   ______
2. What couldn't you do?
   ______
3. What can you do really well now?
   ______
4. What can't you do?
   ______
5. What would you like to be able to do in the future?
   ______

## 2 **VOCABULARY** DIY and repairs, paraphrasing

**a** Complete the crossword.

**ACROSS →**

1 It's a tool with two shaped ends that you use for tightening or loosening small pieces of metal called nuts.
5 It's a tool with a heavy metal head that you use for hitting nails.
6 It's a long thin piece of metal that can carry electric currents or you use to tie things.
8 It's something you use to climb up, e.g. to paint a ceiling.
9 It's an object you could use to stop people from opening a gate.
11 It's an object you use for carrying water.
13 It's a tool you use for tightening screws.
16 It's a tool you use for making holes.

**DOWN ↓**

2 It's a thing you might need to buy if you want to make a piece of furniture, e.g. a table, some shelves, etc.
3 They're made of metal and you can put them in a wall to hang pictures on.
4 They're used to build walls.
7 It's what you use to put paint on, e.g. a wall.
10 They're made of metal and you can use them to fix two things together.
12 It's what you turn to let water out of a pipe.
14 It's a kind of very thick strong string that you use for tying or lifting heavy things.
15 They're things you can use to cover the bathroom wall.

**b** Complete the conversations.

1 A This lamp isn't working.
B Hang on. I'll change the l*ight*______ b*ulb*______.

2 A It's very dark outside.
B Don't worry. I'll take a t______.

3 A How do you lock this door?
B You have to pull the h______ up.

4 A I need to light the candles.
B There's a b______ of m______ in the drawer.

5 A I've bought some wrapping paper for Mary's present.
B Great! Do we have any S______?

6 A I need to stick this photo on my application form.
B OK. Here's the gl______.

7 A How wide is our bedroom window?
B I don't know. Use the t______ m______.

8 A I want to put up this poster.
B OK. Here are some dr______ p______.

9 A How can I tie up this parcel?
B Why don't you use a piece of str______.

10 A This plug doesn't work.
B Oh. You might need to change the f______.

11 A Do you have any scissors?
B No, but you can use my p______.

12 A Can you sew on this button?
B OK, but I'll need a n______ and thr______.

**c** Look at the photos. What are the people doing? Complete the sentences with the present continuous form of a verb from the list. Use contractions.

change drill mend put together
put up set up sew stick ~~tie~~

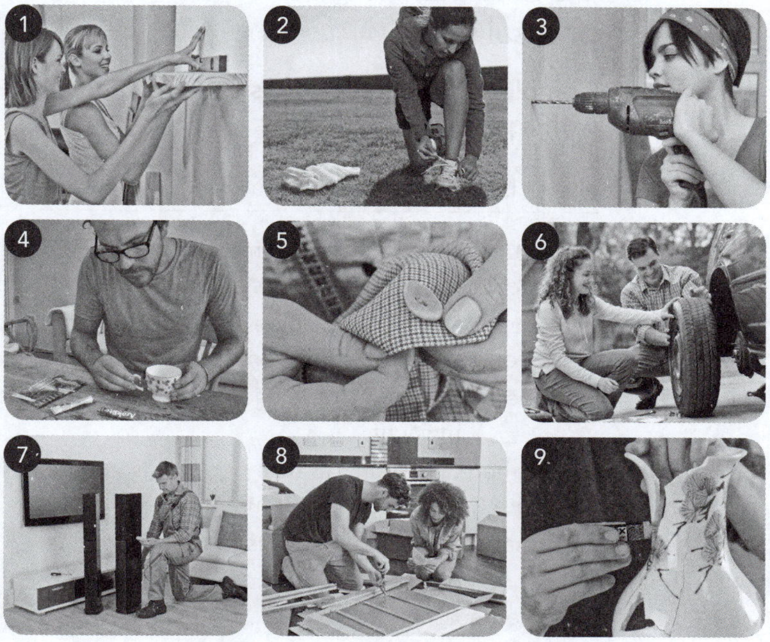


1 They*'re putting up* some shelves.
2 She__________ her shoelace.
3 She__________ a hole in the wall.
4 He__________ the handle on.
5 She__________ a button on a shirt.
6 They__________ a tyre.
7 He__________ a home cinema system.
8 They__________ a cupboard.
9 He__________ a vase.

**d** Answer the questions about you.

1 Who does the DIY in your house?
__________
__________

2 Which DIY jobs can this person do?
__________
__________

3 Have you ever made a piece of furniture? Why / Why not?
__________
__________

4 Which tools do you know how to use? Which would you never use?
__________
__________

5 What things are there in a 'useful things' drawer in your house?
__________
__________

## VOCABULARY FROM READING

Circle the correct word.

1 How long will it take for my skin to *absorb* / *apply* the cream?
2 The museum has removed the painting because they're going to *seal* / *restore* it.
3 If your boots get wet, *stuff* / *crumple* them with newspaper to help them dry more quickly.
4 Can you *restore* / *rub* my back for me? It's hurting again.
5 Don't forget to *absorb* / *seal* the envelope before you post the letter.
6 *Apply* / *Keep away* a layer of sunscreen every two hours when you're out in the sun.
7 Don't forget to *rub* / *rinse* your hair really well when you've used the shampoo.
8 To light a fire quickly, *crumple* / *restore* some pieces of newspaper into a ball and put them under the wood.
9 *Keep away* / *Place* from the edge of the cliff – you might fall.
10 *Place* / *Stuff* the decorations carefully on top of the cake.

## 3 PRONUNCIATION
### consonant clusters

**a** 6.3 Listen and write the sentences.

1 *The new shelves aren't straight.*
2 __________
3 __________
4 __________
5 __________
6 __________

**b** 6.3 Listen and check. Then listen again and repeat the sentences.

# 7A Take your cash

I don't want to make money. I want to make a difference.
*Lady Gaga, American singer*

**G** phrasal verbs **V** cash machines; phrasal verbs **P** linking

## 1 VOCABULARY cash machines

**a** Complete the instructions with the words from the list.

account amount cash enter ~~insert~~
receipt remove select withdraw

### Tips for using a **cash machine**

1 *Insert* your card into the machine.
2 ________ your language.
3 ________ your PIN.
4 Select a transaction, e.g. ________ cash.
5 Select the ________ type.
6 Select or enter the ________.
7 ________ your card.
8 Take your ________.
9 Only print a ________ if you need one.

**b** Replace the **bold** words with a formal word from **a**.

1 Make sure nobody is watching when you **key in** your number. *enter*
2 There's a limit to the amount of money you can **take out** each day. ________
3 It's a good idea to check you can remember your PIN before you **put in** your card. ________
4 If you **choose** the wrong transaction, you can usually go back and start again. ________
5 Most machines don't give you your cash until you **take out** your card. ________

## 2 VOCABULARY & GRAMMAR phrasal verbs

**a** Complete the phrasal verbs in the sentences with a particle from the list.

~~away~~ back off (x2) on out

1 If you won the lottery, how much money would you give *away* to friends and family?
2 When do you think you'll be able to pay ________ the money you borrowed from me last month?
3 None of my cousins have a job; they all live ________ my aunt.
4 Wait here. I'm going to take ________ some money before we go into the restaurant.
5 My salary isn't enough for us to live ________.
6 I'm hoping to pay ________ our mortgage by the time we retire.

**b** Complete the phrasal verbs in the conversations with a verb from the list.

be (x2) call get give put ~~run~~ take

1 **A** What would you do if a big dog ran towards you?
**B** I'd *run* away. I'm really scared of dogs.

2 **A** What shall we do with our old washing machine?
**B** They'll ________ it away when they bring the new one.

3 **A** Are you going out?
**B** Yes, but I'll ________ back in an hour.

4 **A** How long will the car be in the garage?
**B** We'll ________ it back on Friday.

5 **A** Do you know where my blue shirt is?
**B** Yes – I ________ it away in your wardrobe.

6 **A** Can I speak to Grace, please?
**B** She isn't in. Can you ________ back later?

7 **A** Can I borrow your keys? I can't find mine.
**B** Yes, but remember to ________ them back.

8 **A** Is your girlfriend at home?
**B** No, she'll ________ away until Sunday night.

**c** **Complete the conversations with a phrasal verb from the list.**

take after take apart take off (x2)
take on take out take over take up

1 **A** Come in and *take off* ________ your coat. Would you like a coffee?
**B** Yes, please. I'd love one.

2 **A** How many job vacancies are there?
**B** They want to ________ 20 new employees.

3 **A** How are you planning to get fit?
**B** I'm going to ________ aerobics.

4 **A** Who are you most similar to in your family?
**B** I ________ my gran. We even look the same.

5 **A** What are you doing for your husband's birthday?
**B** I'm going to ________ him ________ for dinner.

6 **A** Why are you worried about your job?
**B** I've heard that a bigger company is trying to ________ ours.

7 **A** Which terminal are you flying from?
**B** I'm not sure. Domestic flights ________ from Terminal 3, don't they?

8 **A** Why isn't this clock working?
**B** No idea, Let's ________ it ________ and look inside.

**d** **Complete the sentences with the words in brackets in the correct order.**

1 My boyfriend *picked me up* ________ from the station when I arrived. (me picked up)
2 I've bought a home cinema system, but I don't know how to ________. (up it set)
3 Shall I get the bill, or have you just ________? (for it asked)
4 Your music is too loud. Can you ________, please? (down it turn)
5 I can't find my car keys. Can you help me ________? (for them look)
6 I'm really busy. Can you ________ later? (back call me)
7 We're going to a concert tonight. We're really ________. (forward it looking to)
8 I've bought a new picture. Can you help me ________? (it put up)

**e** **Rewrite the highlighted phrases using a pronoun. Change the word order if necessary.**

1 I don't get on with my boyfriend's mother.
*get on with her*
2 Do you mind if I switch on the lights?
________
3 Please can you take out the rubbish?
________
4 He's going out with my friend's sister.
________
5 I'd send back that steak – it's burnt.
________
6 I've been looking after my friend's children.
________
7 Can you ask for the bill?
________
8 Why don't you try on those shorts?
________
9 Alice is going to move in with her boyfriend next month.
________
10 I'm going to throw away all my old magazines.
________

**f** Complete the text with the phrasal verbs from the list. If there is an object in brackets, put it in the correct position.

get on with ~~grew up~~ look after look for move back move in with pay off settle down ~~take after~~ went out with

I was born in Bristol in the south-west of England, and that's where I [1] *grew up*. There are five of us in my family: my parents, my brother and sister, and me. I'm closest to my dad, and everyone says I [2] *take after him* (him) because we have the same sense of humour. I'm very fond of my mum and my brother and sister and I [3] ________ (them) very well. My sister has two young children, and I sometimes [4] ________ (them) so that she and my brother-in law can go out in the evening.

I left Bristol when I was 18 to go to university in Exeter. In my first year, I lived in a hall of residence, and I made three wonderful friends. In my second year, I [5] ________ (them) – we lived in a lovely old house near the city centre. I took out a student loan while I was at university, and I'm hoping to [6] ________ (it) before I retire!

When I finished university, I [7] ________ (a job) in Exeter, and I was lucky enough to find one very quickly. I met my husband at work, and I [8] ________ (him) for about three years before we got married. We decided to [9] ________ together in Exeter because it's a great place to live and raise a family. I often visit my friends and family in Bristol, but I don't think I'll ever [10] ________ there.

**g** Write a paragraph about your life. Use at least six of the phrasal verbs in **f**.

________________________________________

________________________________________

________________________________________

________________________________________

________________________________________

________________________________________

________________________________________

________________________________________

________________________________________

________________________________________

## 3 PRONUNCIATION linking

**a** Rewrite the phrases with a pronoun. Change the word order if necessary.

1 throw away that cheese *throw it away*
2 put away your shoes ________
3 switch the computer off ________
4 fill in the form ________
5 give away my old phone ________
6 put up the mirror ________

**b** 7.1 Listen and check. Then listen again and repeat the phrases.

**c** 7.2 Listen and complete the sentences.

1 If the children are still asleep, *wake them up*.
2 If you like Anna, ________.
3 If you want to remember the word, ________.
4 If you want to watch the TV, ________.
5 If you don't know the answer, ________.
6 If you don't want that coat, ________.

**d** 7.2 Listen again and repeat the sentences.



Go online for more practice

# 7B Shall we go out or stay in?

> A good film is when the price of the dinner, the cinema admission, and the babysitter were worth it.
> *Alfred Hitchcock, British film director*

**G** verb patterns **V** live entertainment **P** homographs

## 1 VOCABULARY live entertainment

**a** Circle the correct word.

1 Everybody in the basketball *arena* / *stage* was silent before he scored the winning points.
2 The *audience* / *crowd* liked the play so much that they all stood up and clapped when it finished.
3 The players left the pitch at *the interval* / *half-time*.
4 The *spectators* / *fans* cheered loudly when the band came on.
5 We were given a *plot* / *programme* as we entered the theatre.
6 The first *performance* / *scene* of the play is set in an old castle.
7 The only seats left were upstairs in the *stalls* / *circle*.
8 We had an excellent view of the stage, even though we were sitting in the back *row* / *line*.
9 The actor's brilliant *stage* / *performance* in the film won him an Oscar.
10 There was a short *interval* / *half-time* in the middle of the concert.
11 I didn't enjoy that play – I couldn't follow the *plot* / *scene* at all.
12 A *spectator* / *crowd* of about 30,000 people attended the concert.

**b** Read the definitions and write the words.

1 a large building, usually with no roof, where people can sit and watch sport
st*adium*
2 a person who plays against somebody
opp__________
3 the place where the tickets for a play are sold
b__________ o__________
4 the number of points that somebody gets in a game
sc__________
5 the piece of cloth that covers the front of the stage
c__________
6 the sound a referee makes that indicates the end of a football match
f__________ wh__________
7 an afternoon performance of a play
m__________
8 an additional playing period at the end of a match
ex__________ t__________
9 the piece of paper that allows you to attend a play or sporting event
t__________
10 the seats nearest the front of a cinema or theatre on the ground floor
st__________
11 a person who is watching an event, especially a sports event
sp__________
12 a platform in a theatre on which actors, dancers, etc., perform
st__________

**c** Complete the paragraphs with words from **a** and **b**.

# A Midsummer Night's Dream

The last play I saw was Shakespeare's *A Midsummer Night's Dream*. It was on at our local theatre. There was a [1] performance on Saturday and Sunday evening, but we went to the [2] ______ at two o'clock on Sunday afternoon. We bought our tickets at the [3] ______ before we went in. It's a very simple theatre, so most of the seats are on the ground floor in the [4] ______. There are only a few rows of seats in the [5] ______ upstairs. There was a young man selling [6] ______ at the door. The actors were all children, so the [7] ______ was made up of their families and friends. The parents were sitting in the front [8] ______, so we sat further back where we still had a good view of the [9] ______. The play was in two parts and there was a short [10] ______ after about an hour. It followed the basic [11] ______ of the original play, but each actor played three different characters. When the [12] ______ went up, there was a clothes rail at the side of the stage with all their costumes. The actors came on wearing black leggings and black T-shirts. At the start of each new [13] ______, they put on a skirt or a jacket over the black clothes to show which character they were playing. It was an original idea and it worked really well!

**Atlético Madrid 1–0 Getafe**

My Spanish cousins are [14] ______ of Atlético Madrid, and the last time I visited them they took me to a match. The team's [15] ______ that day were Getafe and the match was at the Alfonso Pérez [16] ______ in Getafe. My cousins booked the [17] ______ for the match online. There was quite a large [18] ______ at the match – there were about 15,000 [19] ______. Atlético Madrid were the best team in the first 45 minutes and at [20] ______-______ they were winning 1–0. Getafe played better in the second half, but Atlético Madrid still won. The [21] ______ was 2–1 when the referee blew the [22] ______ after five minutes of [23] ______.

## 2 PRONUNCIATION homographs

**a** 7.3 Listen and complete the sentences.

1 a A panda is a kind of bear.
  b I can't bear cold weather. S
2 a Please ______ the door when you leave.
  b The stadium is ______ to the station. ___
3 a ______ on your back and close your eyes.
  b Is it ever OK to tell a ______? ___
4 a You only need to cook this pasta for a ______.
  b This writing is ______ – I can't read it. ___
5 a Their ______ child was born last month.
  b They won the match in the last ______. ___
6 a My watch has stopped. I forgot to ______ it.
  b The ______ has blown down a tree. ___

**b** 7.3 Listen again. Are the missing words pronounced the same or differently? Write **S** (same) or **D** (differently).

## 3 GRAMMAR verb patterns

**a** Circle the correct form.

1 My friends enjoy *to dance* / *dance* / *dancing*, so they go clubbing every weekend.
2 I forgot *to book* / *book* / *booking* a table, and when we got to the restaurant it was full.
3 We'll have to get a taxi because I can't *to start* / *start* / *starting* the car.
4 It's difficult *to get up* / *get up* / *getting up* early after a late night.
5 My sister hates *not to see* / *not see* / *not seeing* her boyfriend during the week.
6 *To go* / *Go* / *Going* to concerts can be very expensive.
7 We decided *not to cook* / *not cook* / *not cooking* last night and we ate out instead.
8 You must *to wear* / *wear* / *wearing* a suit if you want to make a good impression at your interview.
9 Amy is having a party *to celebrate* / *celebrate* / *celebrating* her birthday.
10 I'm fed up with *to watch* / *watch* / *watching* TV. Let's play cards instead.

**b** **Complete the sentences with the correct form of a verb from the list. Use infinitive with *to*, infinitive without *to*, or gerund.**

be buy enjoy get changed look after
not have not see steal ~~talk~~ walk

1 After they got home, they kept on *talking* ________ until three o'clock in the morning.
2 I don't mind ________ the children tonight so that you can go out.
3 Susan can't afford ________ a ticket for the Rihanna concert.
4 He pretended ________ us because he didn't want to talk to us.
5 Don't wait up for me – I might ________ home late.
6 I ended up ________ home because I'd missed the last bus.
7 I hate ________ a car – I had to sell mine because I couldn't afford it.
8 I suppose we ought ________ before we go out tonight.
9 The man denied ________ my handbag, although it was found in his flat.
10 I didn't expect ________ the play as much as I did.

**c** **Complete the second sentence so it has a similar meaning to the first sentence. Use the past simple form of the verb in brackets and a pronoun.**

1 'Go on! Please go to the party,' my friend said. (persuade)
My friend *persuaded me to go to the party*.
2 'Can you help with the dishes, please?' Tom said to his daughter. (want)
He ________ with the dishes.
3 'You should apply for a promotion.' Sarah's boss said to her. (tell)
Sarah's boss ________ a promotion.
4 'Would you mind decorating the living room?' Mike's wife said to him. (ask)
Mike's wife ________ the living room.
5 'Stop!' the police officer shouted at us. (order)
The police officer ________.
6 'Would you like to come for dinner?' we asked our neighbours. (invite)
We ________ for dinner.
7 'You can stay out until 1.00 a.m.,' said Dan's parents. (allow)
Dan's parents ________ until 1.00 a.m.
8 'You should rest for a few days,' my doctor said. (advise)
The doctor ________ for a few days.

**d** **Complete the questions with the correct form of the verbs in brackets.**

1 Which sport do you most enjoy *watching* ________? Why? (watch)
2 Do you prefer ________ sport or ________ it? Why? (do / watch)
3 Are there any new plays or films that you recommend ________? Why? (see)
4 If you went to the theatre, would you choose ________ in the stalls or in the circle? Why? (sit)
5 Have you ever planned ________ to a live event which was cancelled? What happened? (go)
6 Have you arranged ________ to a live event in the next few months? Which event? When? (go)
7 Have you ever forgotten ________ your tickets to an event? What happened? (take)
8 Which singer or band would you most like ________? Why? (see)
9 Have you given up ________ any sports or hobbies recently? (do)
10 Where can you ________ films in English where you live? (see)

**e** **Answer the questions in d about you.**

1 ________
2 ________
3 ________
4 ________
5 ________
6 ________
7 ________
8 ________
9 ________
10 ________

**Go online** for more practice | **Go online** to check your progress

EPISODE 4

# Practical English Is it a clue?

talking about house rules

## 1 TALKING ABOUT HOUSE RULES

**a** Complete the phrases with a word from the list.

~~anything~~ connect cook course else have mind mustn't need OK problem start think word

1 Is there anything ________ I should know?
2 Could I ________ my laptop
3 Anything ________?
4 you can't ________ meat
5 I don't ________ so.
6 Do you ________ if
7 to ________ with,
8 Of ________ you can.
9 you ________ use
10 That's not a ________.
11 We don't ________ one
12 is it ________ if I use
13 all lower case, all one ________
14 Is there anything you ________?

**b** Complete the conversations with the phrases in **a**.

**A** [1]Is there anything I should know? Are there any house rules?
**B** Well, [2]________ it's a no-smoking house.
**A** [3]________. I don't smoke.
**B** Secondly, we're all vegetarians, so [4]________ or leave meat products in the fridge.
**A** OK. [5]________
**B** No, [6]________ [7]________
**A** There is one thing. [8]________ to your wi-fi?
**B** Sure. The password's 'home', [9]________.
**A** Thanks. And [10]________ your washing machine?
**B** [11]________ The detergent is under the sink.
**A** Right.
**B** Oh, we're trying to save energy, so [12]________ a hot water programme.
**A** That's fine. [13]________ I use your dryer, too?
**B** Sorry. [14]________.
**A** Oh, OK. Is there a washing line?
**B** Yes, there's one in the garden.

## 2 SOCIAL ENGLISH

**a** Match 1–6 to a–f to make Social English phrases.

| | | | |
|---|---|---|---|
| 1 Any | d | a | a mess. |
| 2 Did you | ____ | b | business. |
| 3 I hope | ____ | c | get that? |
| 4 I'll keep | ____ | ~~d~~ | ~~news?~~ |
| 5 It's all such | ____ | e | so. |
| 6 That parking | ____ | f | trying. |

**b** Complete the conversations with the phrases in **a**.

**1** **A** What about your interview? Any news?
**B** I didn't get the job.
**A** That's disappointing.
**B** I know, but ________

**2** **A** Go straight on, take the first road on your right and then the second on your left. ________
**B** Yes, first right and second left.
**A** Do you think you'll be able to find it?
**B** ________

**3** **A** Have you spoken to your neighbours since the argument. ________
**B** Not yet. ________
**A** I know, but you must talk to them about it.

**Go online** to practise the Practical English phrases

# Can you remember...? 1–7

## 1 GRAMMAR

Complete the second sentence so it has a similar meaning to the first sentence. Write 3–5 words. Use the word in brackets.

1 Zach has no money, so he can't buy his own flat. (afford)
Zach ______________ his own flat.

2 Would you like to see what that shirt looks like? (try)
Would you like ______________ that shirt?

3 Swimming in the lake is prohibited. (mustn't)
______________ in the lake.

4 Clare and Debbie met a long time ago. (known)
Clare and Debbie ______________ years.

5 Our mortgage is paid, so this house is ours. (belongs)
We've paid our mortgage, so this house
______________.

6 There's nothing to eat. I need to go shopping. (anything)
If I don't go shopping, we ______________ to eat.

## 2 VOCABULARY

Circle the word that is different.

1 background centre foreground landscape
2 professor thesis tutor undergraduate
3 back up be on switch off turn over
4 hammer light bulb screwdriver spanner
5 cup glass knife mug
6 key in put in take off take out

## 3 PRONUNCIATION

Circle the word with a different sound.

| | |
|---|---|
|  phone | 1 close-up raincoat rope score |
|  owl | 2 crowd pouch show towel |
|  snake | 3 cups forks plates spoons |
|  zebra | 4 batteries lectures references stones |
| /ɪz/ | 5 bushes headphones lenses pieces |

## 4 GRAMMAR & VOCABULARY

Read the article. Circle a, b, or c.

### Fancy coming to a concert... ...at my place?

In the USA, it's becoming more and more common for people to host house concerts. A house concert is a live [1]____ by musicians in somebody's private home. The first step in organizing one is to agree [2]____ the artist which date to hold the event. Once that has been decided, the host can send out invitations to the people he or she wants to [3]____ the concert. On the big day, he or she must make sure there are enough chairs for everyone to sit on. Of course, the host always sits in the front [4]____! When the musicians arrive, they have to set [5]____ their equipment. House concerts are good [6]____ everybody concerned for a number of reasons. First of all, the hosts [7]____ to listen to their favourite band in the comfort of [8]____ home. Secondly, the [9]____ has a more personal concert experience, as the guests can talk to the musicians during the evening. Finally, the musicians have a night off from worrying [10]____ money because they know they're being paid for the concert.

| | a | b | c |
|---|---|---|---|
| 1 | arena | performance | stage |
| 2 | about | on | with |
| 3 | attend | come | go |
| 4 | circle | row | stalls |
| 5 | down | off | up |
| 6 | about | at | for |
| 7 | are able | can | is able |
| 8 | our own | their own | your own |
| 9 | audience | fans | spectators |
| 10 | about | for | of |

Go online to check your progress

# 8A Treat yourself

> You have to treat yourself. Life is too short to deprive yourself of things.
> *Nathalie Emmanuel, British actress*

**G** *have something done* **V** looking after yourself **P** sentence stress

## 1 GRAMMAR *have something done*

**a** Circle the correct form.

1 A I'm going to *have my nails done* / *do my nails* this afternoon.
B Who does them for you?
A My friend, Lisa. She's very good.

2 A Can you take my suit to the dry cleaner's tomorrow?
B But you only *cleaned it* / *had it cleaned* last week!
A I know, but I got oil on it while I was having lunch yesterday.

3 A We're *fitting a new bathroom* / *having a new bathroom fitted* at the moment. My husband's doing it himself.
B That's impressive.
A Not really, he's a plumber.

4 A Do you mind turning down the TV?
B I won't be able to hear it if I turn it down.
A You should *test your hearing* / *have your hearing tested*. It's really loud.

5 A My TV is still broken. I *haven't repaired it* / *haven't had it repaired* yet.
B Have you called the repair service?
A Yes, they're coming next Tuesday.

6 A My sister *painted her flat* / *had her flat painted* last week.
B Did she do it all herself?
A Yes, she did, but I helped her.

7 A These are great photos.
B Yes. Let's *make some prints* / *have some prints made*.
A Good idea. I'll copy them onto a memory stick and take it to the photo shop tomorrow.

**b** Complete the sentences with the correct form of *have something done*.

1 I'm staying with my parents because I'*m having my flat redecorated*. (my flat / redecorate)
2 I got a new passport last week, so I had to ________________ by a professional. (my photo / take)
3 We ________________; we had a wall built instead. (our fence / not mend)
4 How often ________________ your partner ________________ at the hairdresser's? (his hair / dye)
5 Jo bought a picture for her bedroom, but she ________________ yet. Lucy's going to do it on Saturday. (it / not put up)
6 Where ________________ you ________________? It doesn't look very clean. (your car / wash)
7 I ________________ never ________________. I don't believe in fortune telling. (my fortune / tell)
8 The nurses won't mind if we stay in the room while Rob ________________. (his temperature / take)

**c** Write sentences about the people in the photos. Use the correct form of *have something done*. There are two sentences where *have something done* isn't necessary.

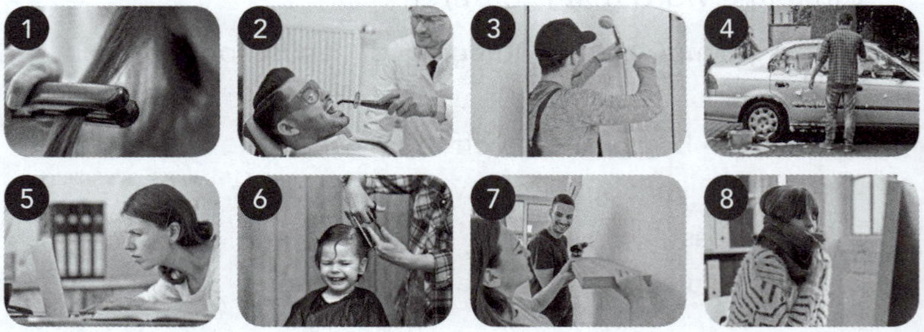

1 she / straighten / her hair
*She's straightening her hair.*
2 he / whiten / his teeth
*He's having his teeth whitened.*
3 they / put in / a new shower
________________________________
4 he / clean / his car
________________________________
5 she / ought to / test / her eyes
________________________________
6 he / not want / his hair cut
________________________________
7 they / put up / some shelves
________________________________
8 she / need / mend / her central heating
________________________________

## 2 PRONUNCIATION sentence stress

**a** 8.1 Listen and complete the sentences.

1 *How often* ______ do you *have* ______ your *car washed* ______?
2 Shall we ______ the ______?
3 ______ did you ______ your ______ ______?
4 We're ______ our ______.
5 I ______ my ______.

**b** 8.1 Listen again and repeat the sentences.

## 3 VOCABULARY looking after yourself

**a** Look at the photos and complete the words and phrases. Write the answers in the puzzle to find the hidden phrase.

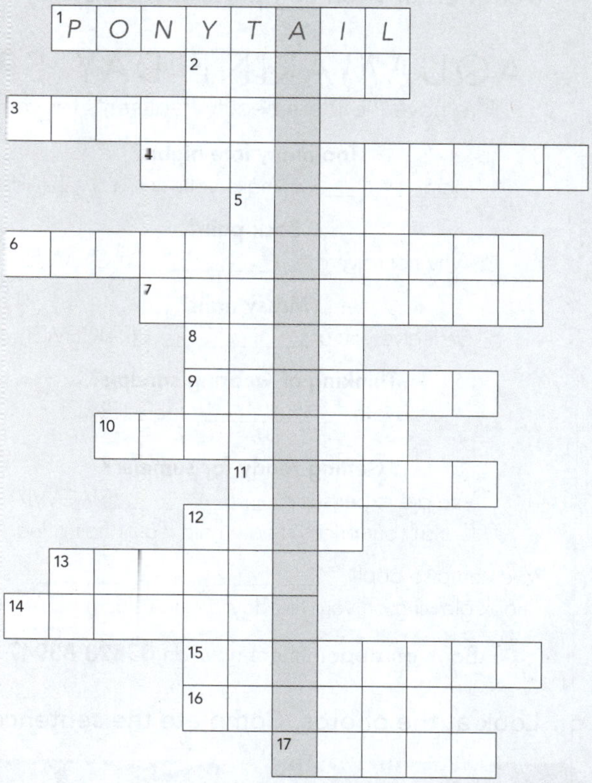

1 a p______

2 have your hair p______ u______

3 a b______ c______

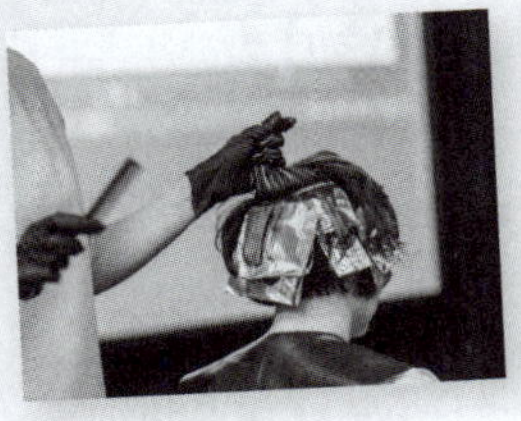
4 have h______

5 have a p______

6 have your hair str______

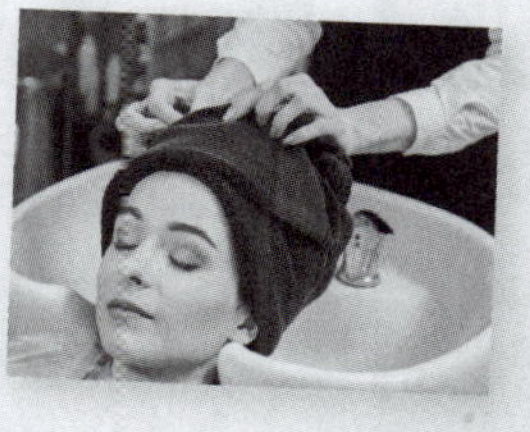
7 have a tr______

8 have a tr______

9 a p______

10 have a bl______ dr______

11 a fr______

12 have your hair d______

13 p______

14 b______

15 have your hair bl______

16 have your hair c______

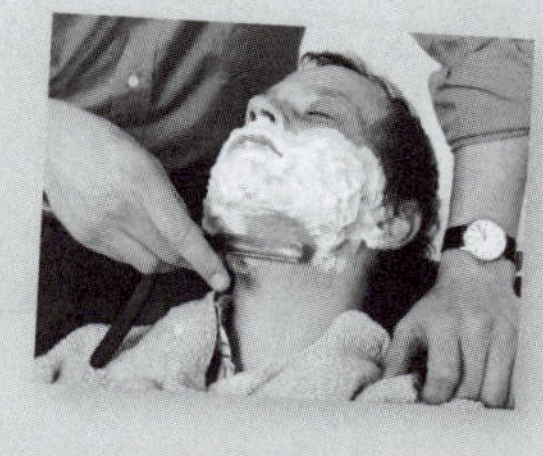
17 have a sh______

**b** Order the letters to make words for beauty treatments. Then complete the advert.

## AQUAMARINE DAY SPA

We have the ideal beauty treatments for you.

**Too many late nights?**
A [1] *facial* ________ will make your skin glow. (CAFILA)

**Back pain?**
Why not have a [2] ____________? (AGSAMES)

**Messy nails?**
We'll give you a [3] ____________. (RAICEMUN)

**Thinking of wearing sandals?**
Have a [4] ____________. (EDUERIPC)

**Getting ready for summer?**
We are experts in [5] ____________. (NAGWIX)
Consult our prices for a whole leg or half a leg.

We can also apply [6] ____________ ____________ so you look glowing on your first day on the beach. (KEAF NTA)

Book an appointment now on **03823 83947**

**c** Look at the photos. Complete the sentences.

1 He's doing sp*inning* ______.

2 She's lifting w____________.

3 He's doing s____________-u____________.

4 He's doing pr____________-u____________.

5 He's using a r____________ m____________.

6 They're using a cr__________ tr__________.

7 They're doing a____________.

8 He's doing P____________.

9 She's doing str____________.

10 They're using an e__________ b__________.

11 She's using a y__________ m__________.

12 She's using a r__________ m__________.

**d** Choose six phrases from the list and write true sentences about you.

change the lock   clean your windows   dye your hair   make clothes   massage your feet   paint your house   repair your car   straighten your hair   trim your beard   wax your legs

1 ____________________
2 ____________________
3 ____________________
4 ____________________
5 ____________________
6 ____________________



**Go online** for more practice

# 8B Sites and sights

History will be kind to me, for I intend to write it.
*Winston Churchill, former British Prime Minister*

**G** the passive **V** wars and battles, historic buildings **P** silent consonants

## 1 GRAMMAR the passive

**a** Circle the correct form, active or passive.

1. The palace *used* / *is used* for weddings and celebrations.
2. Guided tours need *to book* / *to be booked* in advance.
3. Jane Austen *wrote* / *was written* six great novels during her lifetime.
4. The artist *hasn't painted* / *hasn't been painted* a portrait of his wife before.
5. The students *were eating* / *were being eaten*, so we couldn't see the Great Dining Hall.
6. Cameras may *use* / *be used* without a flash.
7. The cathedral is closed to visitors because it *is restoring* / *is being restored*.
8. He enjoys *showing* / *being shown* visitors around the house.
9. We missed the last train because we *had given* / *had been given* the wrong time.
10. The royal family *owns* / *is owned* Balmoral Castle.

**b** Complete the second sentence in the passive. Use *by* where necessary.

1. They built the castle in the sixteenth century.
   The castle *was built in the sixteenth century*.
2. They give guided tours in German, French, and Spanish.
   Guided tours ______________________.
3. You can buy tickets for the play online.
   Tickets for the play ______________________.
4. Has pollution affected the ruins?
   ______________________ the ruins ______________________?
5. They weren't using the hall, so we could go in.
   The hall ______________________.
6. I hate security guards watching me.
   I hate ______________________.
7. They have to handle the exhibits with care.
   The exhibits ______________________.
8. We were relieved that they hadn't cancelled our flight.
   We were relieved that our flight ______________________.
9. The mayor is opening the new museum.
   The new museum ______________________.
10. When are they going to build the new hospital?
    When ______________________?

**c** Complete the text with the correct active or passive form of the verbs in brackets.

Blenheim Palace [1] *was built* (build) as a gift from Queen Anne to John Churchill, 1st Duke of Marlborough. The Queen was pleased with Churchill because his army [2] ______________ (win) the Battle of Blenheim in 1704. Since its completion in 1722, the palace [3] ______________ (be) home to the Dukes of Marlborough, the Churchill – later Spencer-Churchill – family. Former British Prime Minister, Winston Churchill, was born at Blenheim and often [4] ______________ (stay) there with his cousin, the 9th Duke of Marlborough. Today, it's the 12th Duke of Marlborough, Charles James Spencer-Churchill, who [5] ______________ (live) in Blenheim Palace. The park, palace, and gardens can [6] ______________ (visit) by the public. The estate is open all year round except on Christmas Day or when repair work [7] ______________ (do). Each year, there are three tours of the Private Apartments, so that visitors can see the rooms that [8] ______________ (use) by the Duke and his family when they are at home.

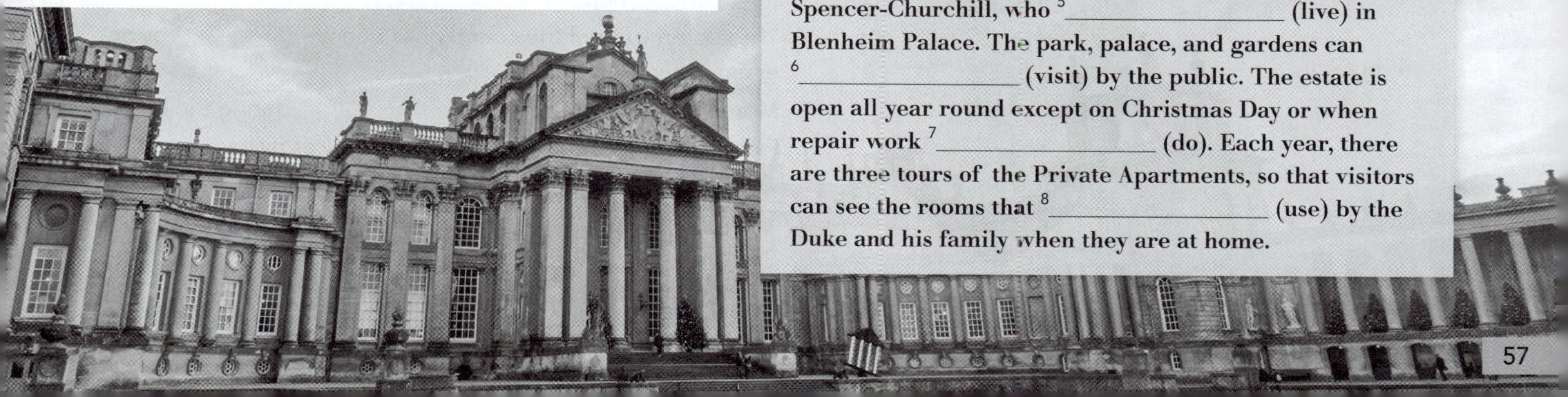

## 2 **VOCABULARY** wars and battles, historic buildings

**a** Complete the labels.

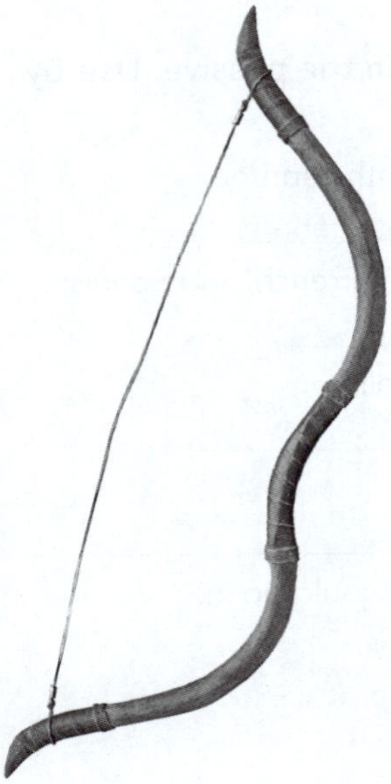

1 b*ow*________

2 arr________

3 ar________

4 h________

5 sh________

**b** Match the verbs from the list to definitions 1–8.

crown defeat destroy ~~fight~~ invade kill retreat succeed

1 to use physical strength, guns, weapons, etc. against somebody *fight*________
2 to make sb die ________
3 to make sb king or queen in an official ceremony ________
4 to win a game, a fight, a vote, etc. against sb ________
5 to move away or back because you are in danger or have lost a battle ________
6 to enter a country with an army in order to attack and take control of it ________
7 to damage sth so badly that it no longer exists ________
8 to have a job or important position after sb else ________

**c** Complete the sentences with the past participle of a verb in **b**.

1 The palace was *destroyed* by bombs during the war.
2 The king lost his crown when his army was ________.
3 When the old queen died, her eldest daughter ________ her.
4 The eastern part of the country has been ________ by an enemy country.
5 More than 5,000 people were ________ during the battle.
6 Fighting has stopped because the enemy army has ________ from the city.
7 The princess was ________ Queen of England when her father died.
8 The battle was ________ between 1861 and 1862.

**d** Complete the labels of the historic buildings.

1 Salisbury C*athedral*

2 Edinburgh C__________

3 Blackpool T__________

4 Whitby A__________

5 Kensington P__________

**e** Circle a, b, or c.

1 Most of the seats are in the ____ of the church.
**a** column **b** nave **c** dome

2 The bodies of the writers Charlotte and Emily Bronte lie in the ____ of their local church.
**a** aisle **b** gallery **c** crypt

3 There are ten rows of seats either side of the ____ of the church.
**a** tomb **b** aisle **c** column

4 There's a ____ along the inner wall of the Main Hall.
**a** gallery **b** nave **c** dome

5 The ____ of many dead poets and artists can be found in Westminster Abbey.
**a** naves **b** tombs **c** aisles

6 The roof is supported by six enormous round stone ____.
**a** columns **b** crypts **c** galleries

7 The ____ of the cathedral can be seen from far away.
**a** crypt **b** dome **c** tomb

**f** Use the words to write questions. Use active or passive.

1 what / the oldest building in your town
*What's the oldest building in your town?*

2 what / it / look like
__________

3 when / it / build
__________

4 what / it / use for / in the past
__________

5 what / it / use for / today
__________

6 what / you / like about it
__________

**g** Answer the questions in **f** about your town.

1 __________
2 __________
3 __________
4 __________
5 __________
6 __________

## 3 PRONUNCIATION silent consonants

**a** 8.2 Listen and complete the sentences. Which consonants aren't pronounced in the missing words?

1 The *castle* is on top of a hill.
2 There's an __________ down the centre of the nave.
3 The historic __________ took place in the main square.
4 The roof is supported by __________.
5 The __________ of the king is in the crypt.
6 He carried a __________ in his belt.

**b** 8.2 Listen again and repeat the sentences.

**c** ~~Cross out~~ the consonants that aren't pronounced in these words.

1 wrapper
2 comb
3 rhythm
4 whole
5 island
6 scissors
7 foreign
8 iron

**d** 8.3 Listen and check. Then listen again and repeat the words.

# 9A Total recall

> Happiness is good health and a bad memory.
> *Ingrid Bergman, Swedish actress*

**G** reported speech **V** word building **P** word stress

## 1 GRAMMAR reported speech

**a** Correct any mistakes in the highlighted phrases. Tick (✓) the correct sentences.

1 She told the doctors that she couldn't remember her name. ✓

2 He said he may forget my birthday, and he did! ✗
*he might forget*

3 Lizzie told her husband that she has never been to Paris.

4 The manager told us it wouldn't happen again.

5 You said you must stay in to study last night.

6 Olga's son told her that he's doing his homework in the school library.

7 I said that I hadn't ever lived abroad.

8 Beth told me that she wrote her dissertation last summer.

9 You said that you won't be late for dinner tonight.

10 My neighbours told me they weren't going to sell their house after all.

**b** Complete the sentences using reported speech.

1 They told us, 'You can stay here until the end of the month.'
They told us that *we could stay there until the end of the month*.

2 He told me, 'I was busy last week.'
He told me that ______.

3 My parents said, 'We've booked a flight for next month.'
My parents said that ______.

4 She asked him, 'Must you go now?'
She asked him ______.

5 Dan said, 'I'm working late tonight.'
Dan said that ______.

6 I said, 'I don't like this restaurant.'
I said that ______.

7 My girlfriend said, 'You didn't call me yesterday.'
My girlfriend said that ______.

8 I asked my boyfriend, 'Are you coming to dinner tomorrow?'
I asked my boyfriend ______.

**c** Complete the sentences using reported speech.

1 'Go to bed.'
Denise told her children *to go to bed*.

2 'Can you give me your phone number, please?'
She asked me ______.

3 'Where did you learn to speak English?'
The interviewer asked me ______.

4 'Do you understand the instructions?'
The teacher asked us ______.

5 'Don't call me at work.'
Lisa asked her boyfriend ______.

6 'What time will you be home?'
My husband asked me ______.

7 'Please make less noise.'
My neighbour asked us ______.

8 'Don't forget your doctor's appointment.'
John's wife told him ______.

## 2 VOCABULARY & PRONUNCIATION
word building; word stress

**a** Circle a, b, or c.

1 It was an ____ goodbye. I don't know when I'm going to see her again.
  **a** emotion **b** emotional **c** emotionally
2 My most ____ birthday was my eighteenth. My parents gave me a car!
  **a** memory **b** memorable **c** memorably
3 I don't know her ____, but everybody else says she's lovely.
  **a** person **b** personal **c** personally
4 My boss stressed the ____ of getting the work done on time.
  **a** importance **b** important **c** importantly
5 He doesn't have the ____ to stand up and say what he really thinks.
  **a** confidence **b** confident **c** confidently
6 Try to report the information ____ to avoid any misunderstandings.
  **a** accuracy **b** accurate **c** accurately

**b** Write the answers from **a** in the correct column.

| Stress on first syllable | Stress on second syllable |
| --- | --- |
| | *emotional* |

**c** 9.1 Listen and check. Then listen again and repeat the words.

**d** Underline the stressed syllables in the pairs of words. Is the stress on the same syllable or a different syllable? Write **S** (same) or **D** (different).

1 memory confidence *S*
2 confident emotional *D*
3 person accuracy ____
4 memorable important ____
5 personally emotionally ____
6 memorably confidently ____
7 importantly accurately ____
8 emotion importance ____
9 accurate personal ____

**e** 9.2 Listen and check. Then listen again and repeat the words.

**f** Match 1–6 to a–f to make collocations.

1 a memorable *d* a announcement
2 an accurate ____ b I think…
3 an important ____ c say that…
4 emotional ____ d occasion
5 I can confidently ____ e intelligence
6 Personally, ____ f description

**g** Complete the sentences with a collocation from **f**.

1 *I can confidently say* Olivia is the best person for the job. You won't regret taking her on.
2 We'd like to make ____________. We're getting married!
3 My colleague is always offending people. He has no ____________.
4 ____________ you should tell her how you feel. Then you can work it out together.
5 She gave ____________ of the thief, and the police caught him the next day.
6 My sister's 21st birthday was ____________ – the whole family was there.

**h** Complete the sentences with the correct form of the word in brackets.

1 A good public speaker has the *ability* ______ to explain his or her ideas clearly and confidently. (able)
2 I'll meet you at the ______ to the museum. (enter)
3 It's ______ that we'll win the match tomorrow. Our best player is injured. (likely)
4 He's been training hard, so he won the race ______. (easy)
5 She doesn't buy anything online because she's worried about internet ______. (secure)
6 Her latest work is an ______ novel. (autobiography)
7 There's an ______ smell in the kitchen. It must be the rubbish. (pleasant)
8 ______ tests are dangerous because radiation is produced. (atom)
9 Most doctors would agree that the ______ between mind and body is important. (connect)

**i** Complete the questions with a word from the list.

forget ~~memorable~~ memorize
memory remember unforgettable

1 What's the last *memorable* ______ occasion you recall?
2 What can you ______ about your first day at school?
3 What was the last number you had to ______?
4 What do you usually do if you ______ someone's name?
5 Do you think you have a good or a bad ______? Why?
6 Have you ever attended an ______ concert? What made it so good?

**j** Answer the questions in **i** about you.

1 ______
2 ______
3 ______
4 ______
5 ______
6 ______

## VOCABULARY FROM READING

Complete the sentences with a verb from the list.

memorize ~~recall~~ remind

1 I can't *recall* ______ the last time we met – was it at your sister's wedding?
2 Please ______ me to get some photos taken – I have to renew my passport.
3 I've tried to ______ our wi-fi password, but it's impossible – it has too many letters and numbers.

Go online for more practice

# 9B Here comes the bride

Always get married early in the morning. That way, if it doesn't work out, you haven't wasted a whole day.
*Mickey Rooney, American actor and comedian*

**G** third conditional and other uses of the past perfect **V** weddings **P** sentence stress

## 1 GRAMMAR third conditional and other uses of the past perfect

**a** Circle the correct form.

1 We *hadn't been* / *wouldn't have been* late if we *had gone* / *would have gone* by taxi.
2 I *had seen* / *would have seen* you if I *had waited* / *would have waited* another five minutes.
3 If Rick *had used* / *would have used* his satnav, he *hadn't got* / *wouldn't have got* lost.
4 If I *had known* / *would have known* it was going to be cold, I *had worn* / *would have worn* a coat.
5 You *hadn't lost* / *wouldn't have lost* your mobile phone if you *had looked after* / *would have looked after* it.
6 Lily *hadn't bought* / *wouldn't have bought* the dress if it *hadn't been* / *wouldn't have been* in the sale.
7 We *had gone* / *would have gone* to their wedding if they *had invited* / *would have invited* us.
8 If you *hadn't left* / *wouldn't have left* the door open, the cat *hadn't got out* / *wouldn't have got out*.

**b** Complete the sentences with the past simple or past perfect form of the verb in brackets.

1 Rob was exhausted because he *'d had* a busy day. (have)
2 It took me a while to find my car because I couldn't remember where I ______ it. (park)
3 My mother told us she ______ well the night before. (not sleep)
4 The children said they ______ hungry, so I made them some pasta. (be)
5 I'd have said 'hello' if I ______ you. (see)
6 One of my aunts asked the bride if she ______ her own dress. (make)
7 I'd tell my friend if I ______ her boyfriend. (not like)
8 The guests said they ______ the meal at the reception. (not enjoy)
9 Jasmine was excited because her sister ______ her to be a bridesmaid. (ask)
10 We wouldn't have come if we ______ you were ill. (know)

**c** Complete the text with the past simple or past perfect form of the verbs in brackets.

## Don't forget the rings...

Last year, my best friend [1] *asked* (ask) me to be the best man at his wedding. I hate weddings, so if he [2] *hadn't been* (not be) my best friend, I would never have agreed! The week before the wedding, my friend took me for a meal and [3] ______ (tell) me what I would have to do on the day. He [4] ______ (give) me strict instructions not to forget the wedding rings.

On the morning of the wedding, I [5] ______ (wake up) late because my alarm [6] ______ (not go off). If I [7] ______ (not go) to bed so late the night before, I might have remembered to set it! My girlfriend arrived to pick me up before I [8] ______ (finish) getting dressed. She [9] ______ (wait) in the kitchen while I put on my suit, then we [10] ______ (drove) together to the town hall.

My friend asked me if I [11] ______ (remember) the rings almost as soon as he [12] ______ (see) me. In my rush to get ready, I [13] ______ (forget) about them completely. It would have been a disaster if my girlfriend [14] ______ (not bring) them. She [15] ______ (see) them on the kitchen table, and she [16] ______ (put) them safely in her handbag. I don't know who was more relieved, my friend or me!

**d** Complete the second sentence so it has a similar meaning to the first sentence.

1 'Nobody spoke to me at the wedding,' my mother said.
My mother told me that *nobody had spoken to her* at the wedding.

2 It stopped raining, then the bride arrived at the church.
When the bride arrived at the church, it ______.

3 We didn't miss the wedding because we took a taxi.
If we ______, we would have missed the wedding.

4 'What time did you get home?' my friend asked.
My friend asked me ______ home.

5 They didn't get married in the castle because it was too expensive.
They ______ in the castle if it hadn't been so expensive.

6 'I didn't have time to call you yesterday,' Lisa said to her parents.
Lisa told her parents that ______ to call them the day before.

7 The venue wasn't very big, so they didn't invite more people.
They ______ if the venue had been bigger.

8 I met the bride's mother at the engagement party, so I recognized her at the wedding.
I recognized the bride's mother at the wedding because ______ at the engagement party.

## 2 PRONUNCIATION sentence stress

**a** 9.3 Listen and complete the sentences.

1 If they'd *known* about the *roadworks*, they would have *taken* the *train*.

2 We would have ______ if we ______.

3 When the ______, she ______ that she'd ______ her ______.

4 You said that you ______ the ______.

5 As soon as he ______ her, he ______ that he'd ______.

**b** 9.3 Listen again and repeat the sentences.

## 3 VOCABULARY weddings

**a** Complete the crossword.

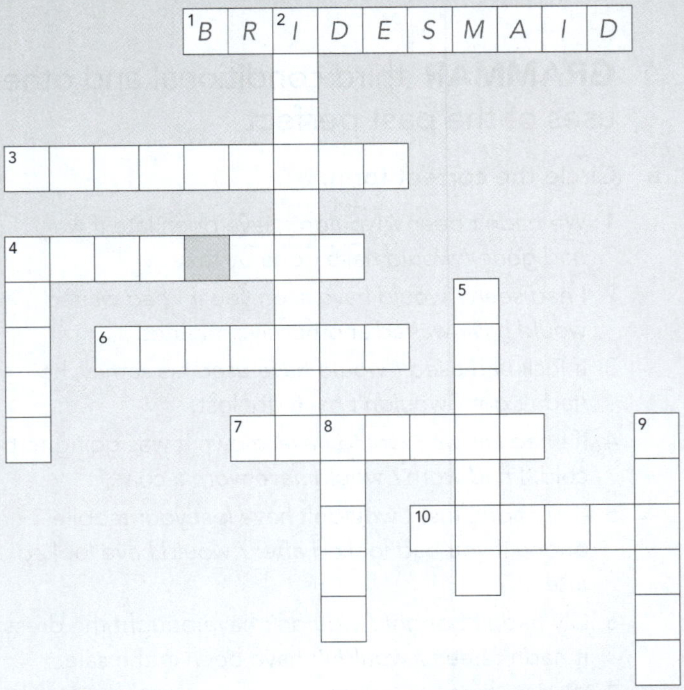


**ACROSS →**

1 a woman or girl who helps a woman at her wedding
3 a party to celebrate a wedding
4 a man who helps and supports the man who is getting married
6 having a husband or wife
7 having agreed to marry someone
10 two people who are together because they are in a relationship

**DOWN ↓**

2 a written request to attend a wedding
4 a woman on or just before her wedding day
5 a small boy who helps or follows a woman at her wedding
8 a man on or just before his wedding day
9 people who are invited to a wedding

**b** Complete the text with the words from **a**.

# A DAY TO REMEMBER

The last wedding I went to was about three years ago. The [1] *bride* was my niece, Rebecca, and the [2] ________ was her partner, Ian. They had been [3] ________ for about six months before the 'big day'. I was very excited when I received the [4] ________ because Rebecca was the first of my nieces and nephews to get married.

The wedding and [5] ________ were held in the same venue – a large country house not far from where they live. They invited about 100 [6] ________ in total. Rebecca had four [7] ________, including her sister, Joanne. Two of her friends' sons were [8] ________. The [9] ________ was one of Ian's friends. He made a very amusing speech when we had finished eating.

It was a lovely wedding. Rebecca and Ian are happily [10] ________, and they make a great [11] ________.

**c** Write a short paragraph about the last wedding you attended. Include...

- when the wedding was and who was getting married.
- how you felt when you received the invitation.
- where the wedding was held and how many guests were invited.
- who played an important role in the wedding.

______________________________
______________________________
______________________________
______________________________
______________________________
______________________________
______________________________
______________________________
______________________________
______________________________
______________________________
______________________________
______________________________
______________________________
______________________________
______________________________

## VOCABULARY FROM READING

Circle the correct adverb and adverbial phrase.

1 I had *never* / *only* been in my hotel room for a moment when I heard voices outside the door.

2 *One morning* / *At last*, I was sitting at my desk when I heard the sound of breaking glass.

3 I'll *never* / *already* trust him again after what he's done.

4 When I arrived, I was disappointed to find that my friends had *after that* / *already* left.

5 After a journey lasting over 24 hours, we reached our destination *never* / *at last*!

6 I got a taxi to the airport, and then I checked in. *After that* / *Already*, I had a coffee and called my mum.

**Go online** for more practice | **Go online** to check your progress

EPISODE 5

# Practical English Finding Henry

giving directions in a building

## 1 GIVING DIRECTIONS IN A BUILDING

**a** Re-order the words to make sentences and questions.

1 Dad's / which / is / room / way
*Which way is Dad's room?*

2 cafeteria / walk / the / the / down / past / corridor
__________

3 the / go / ramp / to / up / main doors / the
__________

4 should / numbers / you / on / doors / see / the / some
__________

5 through / I / them / go / should
__________

6 get / corridor / until / carry / some / stairs / on / you / to / along / the / second
__________

7 you / is / right / sure / way / are / the / this
__________

8 third / towards / of / the / the / corridor / head / end
__________

**b** Complete the conversation with the sentences in **a**.

**Son** Mum, where are you?
**Mother** I'm in your father's room in hospital. Where are you?
**Son** Outside the main entrance. 1 *Which way is Dad's room*?
**Mother** Listen carefully, and I'll tell you. 2 __________. Go through the doors and walk straight ahead.
**Son** It says 'cafeteria'. 3 __________?
**Mother** Yes, I'm sure. 4 __________. Then turn right.
**Son** OK. I'm in another corridor.
**Mother** That's right. 5 __________. Then go up the stairs and turn left.
**Son** OK. I'm walking past the lifts. Why didn't you tell me there was a lift?
**Mother** Never mind about that. Listen. There are some doors after the lifts.
**Son** I've found the doors. 6 __________?
**Mother** Yes, go through the doors.
**Son** Right. Now I'm in another corridor.
**Mother** That's right. You're nearly here now. 7 __________.
**Son** OK...
**Mother** 8 __________. Your father is in Room 212.
**Son** Right...208, 210...Here it is – 212. I'm here! Hi, Dad! How are you feeling?

## 2 SOCIAL ENGLISH

**a** Match 1–6 to a–f to make Social English phrases.

1 Could you fetch *c*
2 Goodness ___
3 I can't ___
4 I just wish ___
5 I must ___
6 It's great ___

a admit,
b knows
c ~~the glasses~~
d to have you back
e wait
f you were here

**b** Complete the conversations with the phrases from **a**.

1 **A** Phew, what a journey! But we're here, at last.
**B** Great. *I must admit,* I was beginning to wonder if we would ever arrive.

2 **A** Sabine and I have got engaged.
**B** This calls for a celebration. __________, Harry?

3 **A** I miss you so much! __________ all the time.
**B** Don't worry, we'll be together soon.

4 **A** This time next week we'll be in Paris.
**B** I know – __________.

5 **A** You're very late. Did you get lost on the way?
**B** Yes. __________ what would have happened if we hadn't had satnav.

6 **A** I'm so happy! __________, Mum.
**B** It's lovely to be here.


Go online to practise the Practical English phrases

fourth edition

# English File

## Intermediate Plus

ONLINE PRACTICE

**Important: Keep this card safe. Before you use your code, speak to your teacher.**

## How to access English File Online Practice

1. Go to: **englishfileonline.com**
2. Choose **Register** to create your Oxford ID.

   OR

   Registered before? Sign in with your Oxford ID and choose **Add a level**.
3. Follow the instructions. Enter your access code.

**You can only use your code once.**

**Need help?** Email Customer Support at **eltsupport@oup.com**

**Your access code**

S-870-450-3423

OXFORD
UNIVERSITY PRESS

ISBN 978-0-19-403904-8

# Can you remember...? 1–9

## 1 GRAMMAR

**Complete the second sentence so it has a similar meaning to the first sentence. Use the word in brackets.**

1 I didn't buy you a present. I didn't know it was your birthday. (bought)
If I'd known it was your birthday, I ________________ a present.
2 'Don't drive so fast,' said Mike's wife. (told)
Mike's wife ________________ so fast.
3 I'm sorry, but I can't go to your party next Saturday. (able)
I'm afraid I ________________ to your party next Saturday.
4 It's raining. They've cancelled the football match. (because)
The football match ________________ the rain.
5 Can I have my tablet back when you've finished with it? (give)
When you've finished with my tablet, please ________________.
6 I've asked the supermarket to deliver my shopping. I couldn't carry it home myself. (having)
I couldn't carry my shopping home, so I ________________.

## 2 VOCABULARY

**Circle the word that is different.**

1 bush gate grass hedge
2 glue nail screw mug
3 curtain half-time stage stalls
4 bunches press-ups sit-ups stretches
5 aisle column nave palace
6 bride groom guest invitation

## 3 PRONUNCIATION

**Circle the word with a different sound.**

| | |
|---|---|
| fish | 1 busy dish fringe visa |
| tree | 2 field hill stream thesis |
| up | 3 butcher's buzz cut jug mud |
| clock | 4 cockerel florist's fold pot |
| horse | 5 couple pour saucer torch |

## 4 GRAMMAR & VOCABULARY

**Read the text. Write one word in each space.**

# Bride misses her own wedding

Nichola met Darren online, they fell in love, and Darren proposed on Valentine's Day.

On their [1] ____________ day, the bride to-be went to [2] ____________ her make-up done at a local department store. When she saw what they'd done, she hated it and rushed home to wash it off. At home, she found that her parents, who didn't approve of the marriage, [3] ____________ decided they weren't going to the wedding. Nichola put her children in the car and drove to a hotel to get ready.

When she arrived, there was a problem with her credit [4] ____________, and when she eventually got into her room, she realized that her daughter's bridesmaid's dress was still at home. With [5] ____________ make-up or wedding dress on, and only half an hour to get ready, Nichola got a text from her adult bridesmaid saying she wouldn't be [6] ____________ to come to the wedding because her child was ill. Nichola burst into tears and called the [7] ____________, who was already at the church with his best man. 'Darren was furious,' she said. When he told her [8] ____________ hurry up, Nichola got even more stressed.

She drove home to get her daughter's dress. But the church was 20 miles away and she knew she had missed the wedding [9] ____________, so she drove directly to the reception for the celebration meal. Unfortunately, when she got there, Darren [10] ____________ her he didn't want to marry her any more. 'It's not the kind of thing you can get over easily,' he said.

# 10A The land of the free?

There is nothing wrong with America that cannot be cured by what is right in America.
*Bill Clinton, American ex-President*

**G** *be, do,* and *have*: auxiliary and main verbs **V** British and American English **P** stress on *be, do,* and *have*

## 1 GRAMMAR *be, do,* and *have*: auxiliary and main verbs

**a** Circle the correct form.

1 Have you ever *been* / *being* on TV?
2 I *didn't* / *didn't do* my homework because I had no time.
3 We couldn't go out. It *is* / *was* raining.
4 *Did you* / *Have you* heard the news? Amy and Ryan are getting married!
5 I can't give you a lift. My car *is being* / *has been* repaired.
6 You're back! *Had you* / *Did you have* a good holiday?
7 *Have you* / *Had you* read the book before you saw the film?

**b** Decide if *be, have,* and *do* are the main verb or the auxiliary verb in the sentences. Write **MV** (main verb) or **AV** (auxiliary verb).

1 New York City **was** briefly the US capital from 1789 to 1790. *MV*
2 George Washington **was** made US President there. *AV*
3 Visitors to New York City can see and **do** hundreds of different things. ____
4 The city **has** over 4,000 street food stalls. ____
5 More than 250 feature films **are** shot in New York annually. ____
6 The New York subway **doesn't** close at night. ____
7 Some of the subway musicians **have** played at Carnegie Hall. ____
8 English **isn't** the only language that people speak in New York. ____

**c** Complete the conversations with the correct form of *be, have,* or *do*.

1 A What shall we *do* tonight?
B Let's stay in. I ________ feel like ________ anything!

2 A Why ________ you at home last weekend?
B I ________ ________ my bedroom painted, so I stayed at my friend's house.

3 A ________ you call me last night?
B No, it ________ me. I would ________ left a message.

4 A ________ you ever ________ aerobics?
B Never. I ________ like ________ exercise.

5 A ________ your car already been repaired when you went to pick it up?
B No, it ________ still in the garage.

6 A ________ you ________ your homework yet?
B No, I ________ still ________ it.

7 A Why ________ your flight cancelled?
B Because of bad weather. They ________ put me on another flight for tomorrow.

8 A ________ you ________ your blood pressure checked recently?
B No, but I ________ seeing the doctor next week.

9 A ________ anyone seen my phone charger?
B Sorry, I ________ ________ using it. Mine ________ working.

10 A ________ you ________ dinner yet?
B No. I ________ know what to cook.

**d** Write the questions.

1 how long / you / have your car
*How long have you had your car?*
2 you / do housework every day
______
3 how long / you / learn English
______
4 you / do any exercise yesterday
______
5 you / ever be to New York
______
6 what / you / do next weekend
______
7 where / be / you / at 10 a.m. this morning
______
8 when / be / the last time you / have your hair cut
______

**e** Answer the questions in **d** about you.

1 ______
2 ______
3 ______
4 ______
5 ______
6 ______
7 ______
8 ______

## 2 PRONUNCIATION stress on *be*, *do*, and *have*

**a** Read the sentences. Tick (✓) if *be*, *do*, or *have* is stressed and cross (✗) if it's unstressed.

1 We aren't going out tonight. ✓
2 When are you going on holiday? ✗
3 She does aerobics to keep fit.
4 Who does the baby look like?
5 I have a friend in New York.
6 Where have you been?
7 Is it going to rain?
8 Why isn't the baby asleep?

**b** 10.1 Listen and check. Then listen again and repeat the sentences.

## 3 VOCABULARY British and American English

**a** Complete the crossword with the American English word that means the same as the British English word.

**DOWN ↓**
1 bill
2 cinema
4 lift
6 toilet
7 trainers

**ACROSS →**
3 secondary school
5 postcode
8 flat
9 rubbish
10 mobile

**b** Write the British English word that means the same as the **bold** American English word.

1 I love the **fall**, when the trees are all different colors. *autumn*
2 When I was a kid, we used to play outside in the **yard** all day. ______
3 Please hang your shirts in the **closet**. ______
4 You can save water if you turn off the **faucet** when you're brushing your teeth. ______
5 The worst thing about flying is having to **stand in line** at the airport. ______
6 Cyclists shouldn't ride on the **sidewalk**. ______
7 Police closed the road this morning because a big **truck** had broken down. ______
8 It was pretty **stingy** of her not to give you anything for your birthday. ______
9 We're running out of **gas**. We'd better stop soon and fill up. ______
10 I left my car in the **parking lot** next to the mall. ______

**c** Read the pairs of sentences and decide which one is British English (**Br**) and which one is American English (**Am**).

1 **a** I live on the first floor, so I always take the stairs. _Br_
  **b** Reception is on the first floor, just inside the front door. _Am_

2 **a** Do you mind paying for the coffee? I forgot my purse, so I don't have any money. ____
  **b** My purse has been stolen – that's my phone, my sunglasses, everything! ____

3 **a** Are you wearing long pants or shorts on the walk? ____
  **b** Have you packed any underwear? You'll need seven pairs of pants for the week. ____

4 **a** There's a subway under the main road – it's the only way to cross. ____
  **b** It's a long walk home from here. Let's take the subway. ____

5 **a** Matt looked so smart when he got married. It was the first time I'd seen him wear a suit. ____
  **b** Harriet was the smartest pupil in the class, so everyone was surprised when she failed the exam. ____

**d** **Write sentences to describe the pictures. Use British English words to describe picture 1 and American English words to describe picture 2.**

**Picture 1**

_The woman at the front of the queue is looking in her purse._

______________________________

______________________________

______________________________

______________________________

______________________________

______________________________

**Picture 2**

______________________________

______________________________

______________________________

______________________________

______________________________

______________________________

______________________________

## VOCABULARY FROM READING

Circle the correct word.

1 Elisabeth Moss is a fantastic actress. I think she's *awesome* / *weird*.

2 OK, I *get* / *nod* it. It's my turn to do the washing-up. You can stop looking at the dishes now.

3 People began eating *compliments* / *turkeys* in Britain in the sixteenth century.

4 My neighbour is really *reserved* / *creepy*. A lot of people are scared of him.

5 I saw her *get* / *nod* when I asked to leave the room, so I knew it was all right to go.

6 I got some *creepy* / *weird* looks when I wore my slippers to school by mistake.

7 You should only pay *compliments* / *turkeys* to people if you really think they look nice.

8 Otto's a bit *creepy* / *reserved* , but he's quite chatty when you get to know him.

Go online for more practice

# 10B Please turn over your papers

Do the best you can until you know better.
Then when you know better, do better.
*Maya Angelou, American poet and activist*

**G** revision of verb forms **V** exams **P** revision of sounds

## 1 VOCABULARY exams

**a** Complete the sentences with a word from the list.

cheat do essay fail multiple-choice oral / speaking pass practical retake revise ~~take~~ true or false written

1 I have to *take* __________ an exam at the end of the course.
2 She was so nervous in the __________ exam that she could hardly speak.
3 I'm going to stay in this evening to __________ for tomorrow's exam.
4 My pen stopped working in the middle of the __________ exam, so I had to finish it in pencil.
5 You can only go up to the next level if you __________ the exam.
6 Candidates have to write a 500-word answer to one of the three __________ questions.
7 I got a really low mark in the exam, so I'm going to __________ it.
8 Answer the __________ questions by writing T or F in the space.
9 We won't know which experiment we have to do in the __________ exam until it starts.
10 Candidates __________ the exam in pairs.
11 It can be helpful to decide which options are definitely wrong in a __________ question.
12 I've got a bad feeling about this exam. I think I'm going to __________.
13 Candidates who __________ in the exam will not be given a final mark.

**b** Complete the texts with the words in **a**. Use the past simple form of the verbs.

After three years of hard work, I remember very clearly how stressed I felt when I [1] *took* __________ my final exams at university. I studied chemistry and I was relieved that the [2] __________ exam was first as doing experiments had always been my favourite part of the course. I was most nervous about the [3] __________ exam – I've always hated that moment before you turn over the paper to start. We had studied so many different topics during the course and I [4] __________ for several weeks before. I was just as worried when it came to the [5] __________ exam. Some people are surprised that chemistry students have to speak in an exam, but it's an important part of most science degrees. It was all worth it in the end though because I [6] __________ everything. However, some of my friends weren't so successful, and they [7] __________ some of the exams later in the summer.

We all know someone who has done something dishonest to [8] __________ in a test or exam. When I was at school, pupils wrote notes on their hand before they [9] __________ an exam or looked to see if the person sitting next to them had written 'T' or 'F' for a [10] __________ question, or had chosen option a, b, or c for a [11] __________ question. I'm a teacher now, and today technology is a big problem with more and more students using devices such as mobile phones and smart watches in exams. There's also a big problem in my school with students who have to write long [12] __________ for their A levels who decide to buy them online instead. One of my pupils did this last year, but they [13] __________ the course anyway because what they paid for was full of mistakes.

## 2 **PRONUNCIATION** revision of sounds

**a** Write the words in the chart according to the pronunciation of the letter *a*.

~~attend~~ campus essay exam fail marks oral pass practical retake seminar similar

| | | | | | |
|---|---|---|---|---|---|
|   | train | 1 |   | car | 3 |
|   | cat | 2 |   | comput**er** | 4 *attend* |

**b** 10.2 Listen and check. Then listen again and repeat the words.

**c** Match the words with the same vowel sounds.

cheat choice could guess multiple ~~option~~ report revise true written

| | | | | | | | |
|---|---|---|---|---|---|---|---|
|   | 1 cl**o**ck | pr**o**blem | *option* |   | 6 **e**gg | t**e**st | |
|   | 2 tr**ee** | dr**ea**m | |   | 7 **u**p | s**u**bject | |
|   | 3 b**u**ll | b**oo**k | |   | 8 b**oo**t | d**o** | |
|   | 4 f**i**sh | f**i**nish | |   | 9 b**i**ke | st**y**le | |
|   | 5 h**or**se | b**oar**d | |   | 10 b**oy** | enj**oy** | |

**d** 10.3 Listen and check. Then listen again and repeat the words.

## 3 **GRAMMAR** revision of verb forms

**a** Circle the correct form.

1 *We have* / *We're having* exams three times a year.
2 *I know* / *I've known* my girlfriend since school.
3 The sun *shone* / *was shining* when I woke up this morning.
4 Be quiet! The teacher *is giving out* / *gives out* the papers.
5 She's staying in tonight because *she's going to* / *she'll* revise.
6 *I had* / *I've had* lunch with a friend yesterday.
7 *I took* / *I was taking* my driving test six months ago.
8 *He spoke* / *He has spoken* to his teacher yesterday about his exam results.
9 *I'm going to lend* / *I'll lend* you my notes if you like.
10 Max couldn't go out because *he spent* / *he'd spent* all his money the night before.

**b** Complete the conversations. Use the correct form of the verb in brackets. Contractions count as one word.

1 A What's the problem with your hotel room?
B It *hasn't* *been* *cleaned* properly. (not clean)

2 A Why are you angry with me?
B Because I asked you ______ ______ the dinner and you haven't. (make)

3 A Can't you stay a bit longer?
B No, I ______ ______ home now. (go)

4 A How old are those houses?
B They ______ ______ in the 1960s. (build)

5 A Your hair looks nice.
B I ______ just ______ it ______. (cut)

6 A Why didn't Jack drive to work this morning?
B Because he ______ ______ his car. (not can, start)

7 A Why don't we go to Australia for a year?
B Because I ______ ______ my job if we did. (lose)

8 A Where did you grow up?
B I ______ ______ ______ on the coast, but we moved to London when I was five. (used, live)

9 A Why is she crying?
B Because her boyfriend said he ______ ______ her. (not love)

10 A Why didn't you speak to Millie?
B I didn't recognize her. If I'd known it was her, I ______ ______ ______ to her. (speak)

**c** Complete the text with the correct form of the verbs in brackets.

The last exam I [1] *took* (take) was my driving test! That was last June. I [2] ______ (already / do) the written test two months before. I was very nervous on the day of the practical exam because I [3] ______ (tell) that the examiner was very strict. He looked very serious while I [4] ______ (drive) around, and he [5] ______ (not say) much at all. But when I [6] ______ (stop) outside the exam centre he told me I [7] ______ (pass)! I [8] ______ (not can) believe it!

Since then, I [9] ______ (drive) my mum's car, but I can't borrow it this week because it [10] ______ (repair). I [11] ______ (buy) my own car if I could afford it, but I don't have enough money yet. I [12] ______ (just / offer) a job with a construction company, so hopefully I [13] ______ (be able to) buy one soon. I [14] ______ (get) a smart car because they're easy to park in the city centre. I probably [15] ______ (not go) on long journeys with my car because petrol is so expensive.

**d** Write a short paragraph about the last exam you took. Include...

- which exam it was, and when you took it.
- how you had prepared for it.
- what happened on the day.
- how the exam will affect your life in the future.

______________________________________________
______________________________________________
______________________________________________
______________________________________________
______________________________________________
______________________________________________
______________________________________________
______________________________________________
______________________________________________
______________________________________________

# 1A

## 1 VOCABULARY

**a** 2 e, 3 f, 4 a, 5 b, 6 d

**b** 2 middle name, 3 maiden name, 4 married name, 5 full name, 6 initials

**c** 2 first, 3 initials, 4 middle, 5 full, 6 married, 7 short, 8 maiden, 9 change, 10 called, 11 named, 12 nickname

## VOCABULARY FROM SPEAKING

2 warm light, 3 simple building system, 4 delicious, 5 brainpower, 6 a wide range of modern colours, 7 Recyclable, 8 good for the planet, 10 click together easily

## 2 PRONUNCIATION

**a** 1 Alex, Sam, 2 James, Kate, 3 Emily, 4 Eve, Leo, 5 Bill, Chris, 6 Caroline, Mike, 7 Paula, Sean, 8 Joe, Sophie

**c** 2 Amy, making, cake
3 Jessica, message, friend
4 Peter, niece, evening
5 Linda, visiting, India
6 Simon, wife, nice
7 George, more, water
8 Tony, going, home

## 3 GRAMMAR

**a** 2 His, 3 her, 4 us, 5 mine, 6 Their, 7 our, 8 them, 9 yours, 10 him

**b** 2 us their tickets
3 you a message
4 them for me
5 me her holiday photos
6 her a suitcase
7 it to me
8 them for you

**c** 2 sent them to her
3 is / 's going to buy it for her
4 sold it to them
5 makes it for us
6 gave it to us
7 is / 's going to get them for us
8 is / 's reading it to him

**d** 2 he, 3 him, 4 it, 5 them, 6 mine, 7 His, 8 it

**e** Students' own answers

**f** Students' own answers

# 1B

## 1 VOCABULARY

**a** 2 compassionate, 3 assertive, 4 thoughtful, 5 loveable, 6 envious, 7 successful, 8 responsible, 9 impulsive, 10 helpful, 11 rebellious, 12 sensitive

**b** 2 possessive, 3 considerate, 4 reliable, 5 glamorous, 6 powerful, 7 creative

**c** 2 impressive, 3 affordable, 4 dirty, 5 dangerous, 6 messy, 7 noisy, 8 recognizable, 9 spacious, 10 comfortable, 11 suitable, 12 luxurious, 13 healthy, 14 peaceful, 15 colourful, 16 restful, 17 stressful, 18 expensive, 19 profitable, 20 desirable

**d** ***-ful* and *-less*:** colourful / colourless, helpful / helpless, hopeful / hopeless, powerful / powerless, restful / restless, thoughtful / thoughtless, useful / useless

**only *-ful*:** peaceful, stressful, successful

**only *-less*:** endless

## VOCABULARY FROM READING

2 g, 3 d, 4 e, 5 b, 6 f, 7 a

## 2 PRONUNCIATION

**a** **Stress on first syllable:** envious, passionate, sensible, sociable
**Stress on second syllable:** desirable, impulsive, rebellious
**Stress on third syllable:** inexpensive, irresponsible, unattractive, unsuccessful

**c** 2 at|trac|tive gla|mo|rous love|a|ble ris|ky
3 in|con|sid|er|ate re|spon|si|ble un|im|pre|ssive un|re|li|a|ble
4 af|ford|a|ble comfor|ta|ble prof|it|a|ble sui|ta|ble
5 af|fec|tion|ate cre|a|tive lu|xu|ri|ous po|wer|ful

## 3 GRAMMAR

**a** 2 those purple flowers
3 taller than her sister
4 as expensive as gold
5 the most reliable person
6 the most intelligent student

**b** 2 more tired, 3 narrower, 4 the least considerate, 5 most stressed, 6 simplest, 7 less expensive

**c** 3 one, 4 one, 5 ✗, 6 ones, 7 ✗, 8 ones

**d** 2 a bit shorter
3 much more polite
4 much more thoughtful
5 much more spacious
6 a bit less active
7 a bit tidier
8 much less stressful

**e** 2 the stupidest / most stupid idea
3 are the smartest ones
4 a bit less sensitive than
5 the one at the end
6 is / 's quieter than
7 are / 're more bored today than
8 the one on the corner
9 is / 's much more sociable than
10 is / 's the most frightened

**f** Students' own answers

# Practical English

## 1 REPORTING LOST LUGGAGE

**a** 2 f, 3 j, 4 i, 5 e, 6 h, 7 g, 8 c, 9 a, 10 d

## 2 LANGUAGE FOCUS

**Type of luggage:** suitcase
**Colour:** greyish blue, light green
**Material:** hard plastic, synthetic material
**Size:** medium size, small
**Extras:** a label, four wheels

## 3 SOCIAL ENGLISH

**a** 1 great, 2 weird, 3 wow, 4 day, 5 miss, 6 awful, 7 take

**b** 1 I really miss you.
2 It's great to see you, too., Oh wow!
3 That's awful., It's not your day, is it?
4 let me take that

# Can you remember...? 1

## 1 GRAMMAR

1 for short, 2 is mine, 3 to me, 4 cheap ones, 5 much further, 6 the least

## 2 VOCABULARY

1 first name, 2 glamour, 3 rebellious, 4 loveable, 5 stressful, 6 messy

## 3 PRONUNCIATION

1 careful, 2 reliable, 3 colourful, 4 compassionate, 5 profitable

## 4 GRAMMAR & VOCABULARY

1 a, 2 b, 3 b, 4 a, 5 a, 6 b, 7 c, 8 c, 9 b, 10 a

# 2A

## 1 VOCABULARY

**a** 2 adaptor, toiletries
3 pack of cards, electronics
4 razor, documents
5 raincoat, things for the beach

**b** **Across:** 5 headphones, 6 scissors, 7 batteries, 10 guidebook, 11 toothbrush, 13 washbag
**Down:** 2 sunscreen, 3 hairdryer, 4 beach bag, 8 towel, 9 underwear, 12 razor

**c** 2 fold, 3 Pack, 4 Wrap, 5 unpack, 6 underwear, 7 washbag, 8 shampoo, 9 scissors, 10 travel insurance documents, 11 booking confirmation, 12 driving licence, 13 passport, 14 visa

**d** Students' own answers

## VOCABULARY FROM READING

2 have the urge
3 get your revenge
4 Whatever the reason
5 develop a magnetic pull

## 2 PRONUNCIATION

**a** 2 shorts, 3 visa, 4 belts, 5 scissors

**c** 2 brushes, 3 sunglasses, 4 cases, 5 boxes, 6 addresses

## 3 GRAMMAR

**a** 2 use, 3 always packs, 4 aren't listening, 5 doesn't usually wear, 6 is always, 7 go, 8 is your girlfriend, 9 speaks, 10 Do you go

b 2 am / 'm going
3 is / 's playing
4 Do, like
5 don't mind
6 are, getting
7 am / 'm flying
8 leaves
9 does, arrive
10 land
11 is / 's picking me up
12 starts
13 are / 're meeting
14 don't want
15 am / 'm, looking forward

c 2 recognize, 3 is / 's thinking, 4 Does it belong, 5 don't want, 6 are / 're having, 7 don't agree, 8 don't believe, 9 doesn't matter, 10 depends

d 2 Who are you going with?
3 Where are you staying?
4 How are you getting there?
5 What do you want to do while you're there?
6 What do you need to pack?
7 Why are you looking forward to it?

e Students' own answers

## 2B

### 1 GRAMMAR

a 2 We didn't go to Kate's wedding.
3 Beth doesn't get on with her boyfriend's parents.
4 The back door of the house is locked.
5 I always sit at the front of the class.

b 3 my mum's birthday, 4 women's clothes, 5 other people's, 6 ✓, 7 ✓, 8 Poppy and Mikey's

c 2 bad habit of his, 3 brother of yours, 4 teacher of Lucy's, 5 idea of theirs

d 2 my own, 3 its own, 4 your own, 5 our own, 6 her own, 7 his own

e Students' own answers

### 2 PRONUNCIATION

a 2 d(r)y cleaner's, 3 g(r)eeng(r)ocer's, 4 haird(r)esser's, 5 garden centre, 6 cha(r)ity shop

c 2 She makes he(r) own clothes.
3 That's my fathe(r)-in-law.
4 Is this you(r) adaptor?
5 We g(r)ow our own vegetables.

### 3 VOCABULARY

a 2 launderette, 3 baker's, 4 jeweller's, 5 stationer's, 6 butcher's, 7 off licence, 8 greengrocer's, 9 fishmonger's, 10 hairdresser's, 11 newsagent's, 12 estate agent's, 13 florist's, 14 barber's, 15 deli
The hidden kind of shop is 'health food store'.

b 2 dry cleaner's, 3 garden centre, 4 travel agent's, 5 craft fair, 6 chain store, 7 car showroom, 8 DIY store, 9 charity shop, 10 pound shop

c 2 looked round, 3 sold out, 4 try on, 5 were out of, 6 closed down

d Students' own answers.

### VOCABULARY FROM READING

2 branches, 3 loyal customers, 4 back in profit, 5 cut costs

## 3A

### 1 VOCABULARY

a 2 toddler, 3 child, 4 pre-teen, 5 teenager, 6 early twenties, 7 mid-thirties, 8 late forties, 9 retired

b 2 pre-teen, 3 in her late forties, 4 Teenagers, 5 in his mid-thirties, 6 Toddlers, 7 in her early twenties, 8 retired, 9 children

c Students' own answers.

### 2 GRAMMAR

a 2 lived, 3 used to have, 4 were sitting, 5 did you stay, 6 didn't use to eat, 7 were you doing, 8 weren't listening, 9 became, 10 Did you use to play

b 2 woke up, didn't have
3 was reading, was cooking
4 didn't wear / didn't use to wear, started
5 didn't have, got married
6 weren't driving, hit
7 lived, was
8 used to go shopping, built
9 lost, were waiting
10 spent / used to spend, were

c 2 used to see / saw, 3 was looking after, 4 were visiting, 5 played, 6 was cooking, 7 called, 8 was running, 9 caught, 10 hurt, 11 didn't think, 12 explained, 13 used to look forward to / looked forward to, 14 could, 15 was progressing

d Students' own answers

### 3 PRONUNCIATION

a /t/ hoped, missed, washed, watched
/d/ changed, lived, played, studied, travelled
/ɪd/ decided, ended, hated, started, wanted

c 2 watch – present, 3 played – past, 4 cooked – past, 5 practise – present, 6 love – present

d 1 play, child
2 played, park, house
3 used, love watching cartoons, home
4 happened, six, family, walking, beach

## 3B

### 1 VOCABULARY

a 2 bottom, 3 behind, 4 top, 5 centre, 6 distance, 7 front, 8 opposite, 9 background, 10 corner

b 2 flash, 3 portrait setting, 4 edit, 5 zoomed in, 6 lenses, 7 out of focus, 8 landscape, 9 overexposed, 10 close-up

c Students' own answers

### VOCABULARY FROM READING

2 cancel, 3 store, 4 upload, 5 go offline

### 2 PRONUNCIATION

a **Stress on first syllable:** photograph, photoshop
**Stress on second syllable:** photographer, photography
**Stress on third syllable:** photogenic, photographic

c (be|hind) bo|ttom cor|ner fore|ground dis|tance

### 3 GRAMMAR

a 2 a, 3 e, 4 d, 5 b

b 2 fell down, 3 swam across, 4 sat down next to, 5 ran along, 6 walked past, 7 climbed up, 8 stood in front of

c 2 to, 3 at, 4 about, 5 for, 6 with, 7 on, 8 with

d 2 looking forward to going
3 told everyone to go
4 succeeded in getting a place
5 believe in having
6 apologized for forgetting
7 entered the room
8 arrived at the hotel

e 2 on, 3 of, 4 about, 5 to, 6 on / over / up, 7 on, 8 for, 9 –, 10 in / inside

f Students' own answers

## Practical English

### 1 LANGUAGE FOCUS

2 family, 3 automatic, 4 satnav, 5 economy, 6 convertible, 7 air conditioning, 8 manual, 9 people carrier, 10 compact

### 2 RENTING A CAR

2 driving licence, 3 kind, 4 door, 5 manual, 6 drivers, 7 models, 8 insurance, 9 charge, 10 parking

### 3 SOCIAL ENGLISH

a 2 afraid, 3 later, 4 tone, 5 Hang, 6 pretty, 7 least

b 1 Please leave your message after the tone, See you later.
2 What's up, at least
3 I'm pretty tired, Hang on.

## Can you remember...? 1–3

### 1 GRAMMAR

1 for me, 2 the least, 3 I'm waiting, 4 their own, 5 use to, 6 fly over

### 2 VOCABULARY

1 slippers, 2 stationer's, 3 roll up, 4 pre-teen, 5 get a mortgage, 6 overexposed

### 3 PRONUNCIATION

1 visa, 2 healthy, 3 jeweller's, 4 attracted, 5 zoomed

### 4 GRAMMAR & VOCABULARY

1 c, 2 a, 3 c, 4 a, 5 c, 6 b, 7 b, 8 b, 9 c, 10 a

## 4A

### 1 VOCABULARY

a 2 surplus, 3 supply chain, 4 food waste, 5 supply

b 2 waste, 3 waste-paper basket, 4 bin bags, 5 bins, 6 refuse collectors, 7 landfill site

c 2 pot, 3 tin, 4 can, 5 jar, 6 tub, 7 pouch, 8 carton, 9 bottle, 10 packet, 11 wrapper, 12 plastic bag, 13 cardboard box, 14 polystyrene tray, 15 sell-by date

d 2 pot, tub, cardboard box, 3 jar, 4 bottle, 5 packet, 6 tin, 7 can, bottle, 8 pot, tub

e 2 reuse, 3 reapply, 4 recycle, 5 replay, 6 rethink

f 2 d, 3 b, 4 a

g Students' own answers

### VOCABULARY FROM READING

2 d, 3 b, 4 a, 5 f, 6 e

### 2 PRONUNCIATION

a 2 sell-by, 3 date, 4 supply

c 3 S, 4 D, 5 D, 6 S

### 3 GRAMMAR

a 3 They'll be, 4 Shall I help, 5 ✓, 6 I won't tell, 7 I was going to, 8 ✓, 9 I'm going to stay, 10 it's going to rain

b 2 shall we do / are we going to do, 3 I'll move, 4 I'll go, 5 Are you going to take, 6 I won't have, 7 I'm going to give, 8 He's going to come round, 9 You won't have, 10 shall I do, 11 I'll help, 12 I won't drop / I'm not going to drop

c Students' own answers

## 4B

### 1 VOCABULARY

a 2 first degree, 3 further degree, 4 Master's degree, 5 PhD, 6 overseas students, 7 tutorials

b **Across:** 4 webinar, 8 lecture, 10 thesis, 11 undergraduate, 12 faculty
**Down:** 2 dissertation, 3 campus, 5 seminar, 6 professor, 7 postgraduate, 9 tutor

c 2 a grant, 3 job offer, 4 covering letter, 5 a scholarship, 6 internship, 7 qualifications, 8 attend

d 2 qualifications, 3 experience, 4 internship, 5 skills, 6 CV, 7 reference, 8 covering letter, 9 attend, 10 intern

### VOCABULARY FROM READING

2 pocket money, 3 earned, 4 wages, 5 checkout

### 2 PRONUNCIATION

a **Stress on first syllable:** reference, residence, scholarship, seminar, vacancy
**Stress on second syllable:** degree, postgraduate, professor, tutorial
**Stress on third syllable:** dissertation, PhD, undergraduate

### 3 GRAMMAR

a 2 g, 3 b, 4 h, 5 a, 6 f, 7 c, 8 d

b
3 we wouldn't complain
4 ✓
5 if we don't work late
6 ✓
7 unless they agree to his conditions
8 He'll do a postgraduate course
9 if I was / were a student
10 ✓

c
2 I earned more money
3 can't go to
4 Matt would live in a hall of residence
5 might do a Master's degree
6 I were you
7 you wouldn't miss your lectures
8 they'll get into trouble

d Students' own answers

## 5A

### 1 VOCABULARY

a
2 cookery programme
3 the weather forecast
4 current affairs programme
5 cartoon
6 documentary

b 2 advert, 3 live sport, 4 reality show, 5 period drama, 6 chat show, 7 the news

c 2 episode, 3 series, 4 soap, 5 box set, 6 seasons, 7 streaming service

d 2 a, 3 f, 4 b, 5 c, 6 e

e Students' own answers

### VOCABULARY FROM LISTENING

2 binge-watched, 3 catch-up, 4 two-screen, 5 streaming, 6 channels, 7 device

### 2 PRONUNCIATION

a 2 bake, 3 van, 4 born, 5 bin, 6 verse, 7 very, 8 best

c
2 voted, best band
3 visited Vietnam
4 watch, quiz, Wednesday
5 volleyball, valuable victory
6 very busy, business

### 3 GRAMMAR

a 3 has just finished, 4 for 20 years, 5 ✓, 6 Have you ever been, 7 ✓, 8 have known each other, 9 ✓, 10 Hasn't the news started yet?

b 2 has just been, 3 I didn't want, 4 I haven't watched, 5 has been on, 6 I've already read, 7 all day, 8 for a month

c
2 has / 's had his speakers for
3 have / 've just got
4 Have you been to Spain
5 have / 've moved house three times
6 have / 've never liked
7 got married ten years ago
8 have / 've already had one

d Students' own answers

## 5B

### 1 VOCABULARY

a 2 hill, 3 valley, 4 stream, 5 bush, 6 gate, 7 lake, 8 field, 9 cliff, 10 well, 11 stones, 12 fence, 13 grass, 14 branch, 15 sticks, 16 hedge, 17 mud, 18 rocks, 19 path, 20 leaf

b 2 planted, 3 tractor, 4 sheep, 5 cockerel, 6 cow, 7 grow, 8 farmhouse, 9 barn, 10 wheat, 11 crops, 12 donkey, 13 lambs, 14 pick, 15 harvested, 16 hens

c 2 fences, 3 Crops, 4 wheat, 5 ripe, 6 grass, 7 cows, 8 lambs, 9 tractor, 10 barn, 11 hens, 12 cockerel

d Students' own answers

### 2 PRONUNCIATION

a 2 hill, 3 earth, 4 harvest, 5 warn, 6 grass, 7 stones, 8 mud, 9 grow

c
2 eating, healthily
3 painting, house
4 haven't, drinking, coffee
5 haven't, watching, series
6 haven't, sleeping, recently

### 3 GRAMMAR

a
2 's been studying
3 have, been driving
4 hasn't been feeling
5 've been arguing
6 've been looking forward to
7 has, been playing
8 haven't been going

b
2 've been going
3 's been walking
4 've been using
5 've been drinking
6 haven't been eating
7 've been swimming
8 has / 's been playing
9 has / 's been making
10 hasn't been adding

c
2 has / 's been living in Paris for two years
3 have been going out (together) for a year
4 has / 's been studying since she came home
5 have / 've been training for three weeks
6 has / 's been raining since eight o'clock

d Students' own answers

## Practical English

### 1 MAKING A POLICE REPORT

**a** b Did you notice anything unusual about her?
c How long has your aunt been missing?
d Where were you?
e Can you describe her?
f Was there anything unusual about the house tonight?
g Can you give me some idea of her normal routine?
h When did you last see her?
i Do you remember what she was wearing?
j Is there anything else?

**b** 2 e, 3 h, 4 d, 5 i, 6 b, 7 a, 8 g, 9 f, 10 j

### 2 SOCIAL ENGLISH

**a** 2 letting, 3 carefully, 4 message, 5 idea, 6 mean

**b** 2 listen carefully
3 What does it mean?
4 I'm all right.
5 It's a message from
6 Thanks for letting me stay.

## Can you remember...? 1–5

### 1 GRAMMAR

1 much older than, 2 friend of mine, 3 were you doing, 4 shall we go, 5 could have, 6 been driving for

### 2 VOCABULARY

1 zoom in, 2 healthy, 3 bin, 4 dissertation, 5 dissertation, 6 gate

### 3 PRONUNCIATION

1 height, 2 replay, 3 vacancy, 4 campus, 5 cartoon

### 4 GRAMMAR & VOCABULARY

1 c, 2 c, 3 b, 4 b, 5 a, 6 c, 7 c, 8 a, 9 b, 10 a

## 6A

### 1 VOCABULARY

**a** 2 oil and vinegar, 3 candle, 4 cup, 5 serving dish, 6 fork, 7 napkin, 8 salt and pepper, 9 teaspoon, 10 glass

**b** 2 bowl, 3 corkscrew, 4 jug, 5 tablecloth, 6 teapot, 7 wine glass, 8 knife, 9 spoon, 10 saucer, 11 tray

**c** 2 c, 3 b, 4 b, 5 a

**d** 2 booked, 3 cleared, 4 took, 5 served, 6 poured, 7 ordered, 8 tried, 9 sent, back, 10 carried, 11 asked for, 12 left

**e** Students' own answers

### VOCABULARY FROM READING

2 overworked, 3 overcooked, 4 understaffed

### 2 PRONUNCIATION

**a** 2 d, 3 a, 4 f, 5 c, 6 e

**c** 2 fish and chips, 3 bread and butter, 4 oil and vinegar, 5 cup and saucer

### 3 GRAMMAR

**a** 2 a, 3 f, 4 g, 5 e, 6 d, 7 c

**b** 2 a, c, 3 a, b, 4 a, b, 5 b, c, 6 a, b, 7 a, c

**c** 2 mustn't make a noise
3 must / have to wear a helmet
4 don't have to / needn't / don't need to iron
5 should / ought to order the steak
6 don't have to / don't need to pay
7 must / have to take used batteries
8 mustn't / shouldn't / oughtn't to let children play

**d** Students' own answers

## 6B

### 1 GRAMMAR

**a** 3 ✓, 4 ✓, 5 can't, 6 ✓, 7 be able to, 8 ✓, 9 been able to, 10 ✓, 11 was able to, 12 not being able to

**b** 3 Can I sit here?
4 I couldn't reply sooner.
I haven't been able to reply sooner.
5 She couldn't finish the meal.
She wasn't able to finish the meal.
6 They want to be able to cook their own meals.
7 That can't be John.
8 We're delighted that we can come to dinner.
We're delighted that we're able to come to dinner.
9 I love being able to get up late in the holidays.
10 We were able to book a room with a sea view.

**c** Students' own answers

### 2 VOCABULARY

**a** **Across:** 5 hammer, 6 wire, 8 ladder, 9 padlock, 11 bucket, 13 screwdriver, 16 drill
**Down:** 2 piece of wood, 3 nails, 4 bricks, 7 paintbrush, 10 screws, 12 tap, 14 rope, 15 tiles

**b** 2 torch, 3 handle, 4 box of matches, 5 Sellotape, 6 glue, 7 tape measure, 8 drawing pins, 9 string, 10 fuse, 11 penknife, 12 needle and thread

**c** 2 's tying, 3 's drilling, 4 's sticking, 5 's sewing, 6 're changing, 7 's setting up, 8 're putting together, 9 's mending

**d** Students' own answers

### VOCABULARY FROM READING

2 restore, 3 stuff, 4 rub, 5 seal, 6 Apply, 7 rinse, 8 crumple, 9 Keep away, 10 Place

### 3 PRONUNCIATION

**a** 2 She changed the bulbs in all the lamps
3 I need a paintbrush and some paint
4 We used some string to mend the handle
5 They got stressed assembling the new cupboards
6 The needles are in my sewing box

## 7A

### 1 VOCABULARY

**a** 2 Select, 3 Enter, 4 withdraw, 5 account, 6 amount, 7 Remove, 8 cash, 9 receipt

**b** 2 withdraw, 3 insert, 4 select, 5 remove

### 2 VOCABULARY & GRAMMAR

**a** 2 back, 3 off, 4 out, 5 on, 6 off

**b** 2 take, 3 be, 4 get, 5 put, 6 call, 7 give, 8 be

**c** 2 take on, 3 take up, 4 take after, 5 take, out, 6 take over, 7 take off, 8 take, apart

**d** 2 set it up, 3 asked for it, 4 turn it down, 5 look for them, 6 call me back, 7 looking forward to it, 8 put it up

**e** 2 switch them on, 3 take it out, 4 going out with her, 5 send it back, 6 looking after them, 7 ask for it, 8 try them on, 9 move in with him, 10 throw them (all) away

**f** 3 get on with them, 4 look after them, 5 moved in with them, 6 pay it off, 7 looked for a job, 8 went out with him, 9 settle down, 10 move back

**g** Students' own answers

### 3 PRONUNCIATION

**a** 2 put them away, 3 switch it off, 4 fill it in, 5 give it away, 6 put it up

**c** 2 ask her out, 3 write it down, 4 turn it on, 5 make it up, 6 give it away

## 7B

### 1 VOCABULARY

**a** 2 audience, 3 half-time, 4 fans, 5 programme, 6 scene, 7 circle, 8 row, 9 performance, 10 interval, 11 plot, 12 crowd

**b** 2 opponent, 3 box office, 4 score, 5 curtain, 6 final whistle, 7 matinee, 8 extra time, 9 ticket, 10 stalls, 11 spectator, 12 stage

**c** 2 matinee, 3 box office, 4 stalls, 5 circle, 6 programmes, 7 audience, 8 row, 9 stage, 10 interval, 11 plot, 12 curtain, 13 scene, 14 fans, 15 opponents, 16 stadium, 17 tickets, 18 crowd, 19 spectators, 20 half time, 21 score, 22 final whistle, 23 extra time

### 2 PRONUNCIATION

**a** 2 close (D), 3 lie (S), 4 minute (D), 5 second (S), 6 wind (D)

### 3 GRAMMAR

**a** 2 to book, 3 start, 4 to get up, 5 not seeing, 6 Going, 7 not to cook, 8 wear, 9 to celebrate, 10 watching

**b** 2 looking after, 3 to buy, 4 not to see, 5 be, 6 walking, 7 not having, 8 to get changed, 9 stealing, 10 to enjoy

**c** 2 wanted her to help
3 told her to apply for
4 asked him to decorate
5 ordered us to stop
6 invited them / our neighbours to come
7 allowed him to stay out
8 advised me to rest

**d** 2 doing, watching, 3 seeing, 4 to sit, 5 to go, 6 to go, 7 to take, 8 to see, 9 doing, 10 see

**e** Students' own answers

## Practical English

### 1 TALKING ABOUT HOUSE RULES

**a** 2 connect, 3 else, 4 cook, 5 think, 6 mind, 7 start, 8 course, 9 mustn't, 10 problem, 11 have, 12 OK, 13 word, 14 need

**b** 2 to start with,
3 That's not a problem.
4 you can't cook meat
5 Anything else?
6 I don't think so
7 Is there anything you need?
8 Could I connect my laptop
9 all lower case, all one word
10 is it OK if I use
11 Of course you can.
12 you mustn't use
13 Do you mind if
14 We don't have one.

### 2 SOCIAL ENGLISH

**a** 2 c, 3 e, 4 f, 5 a, 6 b

**b** 1 I'll keep trying.
2 Did you get that? I hope so.
3 that parking business. It's all such a mess.

## Can you remember...? 1–7

### 1 GRAMMAR

1 can't afford to buy, 2 to try on, 3 You mustn't swim, 4 have known each other for, 5 belongs to us, 6 won't have anything

### 2 VOCABULARY

1 landscape, 2 thesis, 3 back up, 4 light bulb, 5 knife, 6 take off

### 3 PRONUNCIATION

1 score, 2 show, 3 spoons, 4 lectures, 5 headphones

### 4 GRAMMAR & VOCABULARY

1 b, 2 c, 3 a, 4 b, 5 c, 6 c, 7 a, 8 b, 9 a, 10 a

## 8A

### 1 GRAMMAR

**a** 2 had it cleaned
3 fitting a new bathroom
4 have your hearing tested
5 haven't had it repaired
6 painted her flat
7 have some prints made

**b** 2 have my photo taken
3 didn't have our fence mended
4 does, have his hair dyed
5 hasn't had it put up
6 did, have your car washed
7 have / 've, had my fortune told
8 's having / has his temperature taken

**c** 3 They're having a new shower put in.
4 He's cleaning his car.
5 She ought to have her eyes tested.
6 He doesn't want to have his hair cut.
7 They're putting up some shelves.
8 She needs to have her central heating mended.

### 2 PRONUNCIATION

**a** 2 have, shopping delivered
3 When, have, hair curled
4 having, front door painted
5 love having, head massaged

### 3 VOCABULARY

**a** 2 put up, 3 buzz cut, 4 highlights, 5 perm, 6 straightened, 7 treatment, 8 trim, 9 parting, 10 blow dry, 11 fringe, 12 dyed, 13 plaits, 14 bunches, 15 bleached, 16 curled, 17 shave
The hidden phrase is 'at the hairdresser's'.

**b** 2 massage, 3 manicure, 4 pedicure, 5 waxing, 6 fake tan

**c** 2 weights, 3 sit-ups, 4 press-ups, 5 running machine, 6 cross trainer, 7 aerobics, 8 Pilates, 9 stretches, 10 exercise bike, 11 yoga mat, 12 rowing machine

**d** Students' own answers

## 8B

### 1 GRAMMAR

**a** 2 to be booked, 3 wrote, 4 hasn't painted, 5 were eating, 6 be used, 7 is being restored, 8 showing, 9 had been given, 10 owns

**b** 2 are given in German, French, and Spanish
3 can be bought online
4 Have, been affected by pollution
5 wasn't being used, so we could go in
6 being watched by security guards
7 have to be handled with care
8 hadn't been cancelled
9 is being opened by the mayor
10 is the new hospital going to be built

**c** 2 won / had won, 3 has been, 4 stayed, 5 lives, 6 be visited, 7 is / 's being done, 8 are used

### 2 VOCABULARY

**a** 2 arrow, 3 archer, 4 helmet, 5 shield

**b** 2 kill, 3 crown, 4 defeat, 5 retreat, 6 invade, 7 destroy, 8 succeed

**c** 2 defeated, 3 succeeded, 4 invaded, 5 killed, 6 retreated, 7 crowned, 8 fought

**d** 2 Castle, 3 Tower, 4 Abbey, 5 Palace

**e** 2 c, 3 b, 4 a, 5 b, 6 a, 7 b

**f** 2 What does it look like?
3 When was it built?
4 What was it used for in the past?
5 What is it used for today?
6 What do you like about it?

**g** Students' own answers.

### 3 PRONUNCIATION

**a** 2 aisle, s
3 fight, gh
4 columns, n
5 tomb, b
6 knife, k

**c** 2 com~~b~~, 3 r~~h~~ythm, 4 ~~w~~hole, 5 i~~s~~land, 6 s~~c~~issors, 7 forei~~g~~n, 8 i~~r~~on

## 9A

### 1 GRAMMAR

**a** 3 she had never been, 4 ✓, 5 you had to stay in to study, 6 he was doing his homework, 7 ✓, 8 she had written, 9 you wouldn't be late, 10 ✓

**b** 2 he had / 'd been busy the week before
3 they had / 'd booked a flight for the next month / the following month
4 if he had to go then
5 he was working late that night / evening
6 I didn't like that restaurant
7 I hadn't called her the day before / the previous day
8 if he was coming to dinner the next day / the following day

**c** 2 to give her my phone number
3 where I had learned to speak English
4 if we understood the instructions
5 not to call her at work
6 what time I would be home
7 to make less noise
8 not to forget his doctor's appointment

### 2 VOCABULARY & PRONUNCIATION

**a** 2 b, 3 c, 4 a, 5 a, 6 c

**b** **Stress on the first syllable:** memorable, personally, confidence, accurately
**Stress on the second syllable:** importance

**d**

| | | | |
|---|---|---|---|
| 3 | person | accuracy | S |
| 4 | memorable | important | D |
| 5 | personally | emotionally | D |
| 6 | memorably | confidently | S |
| 7 | importantly | accurately | D |
| 8 | emotion | importance | S |
| 9 | accurate | personal | S |

**f** 2 f, 3 a, 4 e, 5 c, 6 b

**g** 2 an important announcement
3 emotional intelligence
4 Personally, I think
5 an accurate description
6 a memorable occasion

**h** 2 entrance, 3 unlikely, 4 easily, 5 security, 6 autobiographical, 7 unpleasant, 8 Atomic, 9 connection

**i** 2 remember, 3 memorize, 4 forget, 5 memory, 6 unforgettable

**j** Students' own answers

## VOCABULARY FROM READING

2 remind, 3 memorize

# 9B

## 1 GRAMMAR

a 2 would have seen, had waited
3 had used, wouldn't have got
4 had known, would have worn
5 wouldn't have lost, had looked after
6 wouldn't have bought, hadn't been
7 would have gone, had invited
8 hadn't left, wouldn't have got out

b 2 had / 'd parked, 3 hadn't slept, 4 were, 5 had / 'd seen, 6 had / 'd made, 7 didn't like, 8 hadn't enjoyed, 9 had asked, 10 had / 'd known

c 3 told, 4 gave, 5 woke up, 6 hadn't gone off, 7 hadn't gone, 8 had / 'd finished, 9 waited, 10 drove, 11 had / 'd remembered, 12 saw, 13 had / 'd forgotten, 14 hadn't brought, 15 had / 'd seen, 16 had / 'd put

d 2 had stopped raining
3 hadn't taken a taxi
4 what time I had / 'd got
5 would / 'd have got married
6 she hadn't had time
7 would / 'd have invited more people
8 I had / 'd met her

## 2 PRONUNCIATION

a 2 arrived on time, hadn't got lost
3 bride arrived, realized, forgotten, flowers
4 hadn't received, invitation
5 saw, knew, done something wrong

## 3 VOCABULARY

a **Across:** 3 reception, 4 best man, 6 married, 7 engaged, 10 couple
**Down:** 2 invitation, 4 bride, 5 pageboy, 8 groom, 9 guests

b 2 groom, 3 engaged, 4 invitation, 5 reception, 6 guests, 7 bridesmaids, 8 pageboys, 9 best man, 10 married, 11 couple

c Students' own answers

## VOCABULARY FROM READING

2 One morning, 3 never, 4 already, 5 at last, 6 After that

# Practical English

## 1 GIVING DIRECTIONS IN A BUILDING

a 2 Walk down the corridor past the cafeteria
3 Go up the ramp to the main doors
4 You should see some numbers on the doors
5 Should I go through them
6 Carry on along the second corridor until you get to some stairs
7 Are you sure this is the right way
8 Head towards the end of the third corridor

b 2 Go up the ramp to the main doors
3 Are you sure this is the right way
4 Walk down the corridor past the cafeteria
5 Carry on along the second corridor until you get to some stairs
6 Should I go through them
7 Head towards the end of the third corridor
8 You should see some numbers on the doors

## 2 SOCIAL ENGLISH

a 2 b, 3 e, 4 f, 5 a, 6 d

b 2 Could you fetch the glasses
3 I just wish you were here
4 I can't wait
5 Goodness knows
6 It's great to have you back

# Can you remember...? 1–9

## 1 GRAMMAR

1 would / 'd have bought you
2 told him not to drive
3 won't be able to go / 'm not able to go
4 has been cancelled because of
5 give it back to me
6 am / 'm having it delivered

## 2 VOCABULARY

1 gate, 2 mug, 3 half-time, 4 bunches, 5 palace, 6 invitation

## 3 PRONUNCIATION

1 visa, 2 hill, 3 butcher's, 4 fold, 5 couple

## 4 GRAMMAR & VOCABULARY

1 wedding, 2 have, 3 had, 4 card, 5 no, 6 able, 7 groom, 8 to, 9 ceremony, 10 told

# 10A

## 1 GRAMMAR

a 2 didn't do, 3 was, 4 Have you, 5 is being, 6 Did you have, 7 Had you

b 3 MV, 4 MV, 5 AV, 6 AV, 7 AV, 3 MV

c 1 don't, doing
2 weren't, was having
3 Did, wasn't, have
4 Have, done, don't, doing
5 Had, was
6 Have, done, am / 'm, doing
7 was, have / 've
8 Have, had, am / 'm
9 Has, have / 've been, isn't
10 Have, had, didn't / don't

d 2 Do you do housework every day
3 How long have you been learning English
4 Did you do any exercise yesterday
5 Have you ever been to New York
6 What are you doing / going to do next weekend
7 Where were you at 10 a.m. this morning
8 When was the last time you had your hair cut

e Students' own answers

## 2 PRONUNCIATION

a 3 ✗, 4 ✗, 5 ✗, 6 ✗, 7 ✗, 8 ✓

## 3 VOCABULARY

a **Down:** 2 movie theater, 4 elevator, 6 restroom, 7 sneakers
**Across:** 3 high school, 5 zip code, 8 apartment, 9 garbage, 10 cell phone

b 2 garden, 3 wardrobe, 4 tap, 5 queue, 6 pavement, 7 lorry, 8 mean, 9 petrol, 10 car park

c 2a Br, 2b Am, 3a Am, 3b Br, 4a Br, 4b Am, 5a Br, 5b Am

d Students' own answers

## VOCABULARY FROM READING

2 get, 3 turkeys, 4 creepy, 5 nod, 6 weird, 7 compliments, 8 reserved

# 10B

## 1 VOCABULARY

a 2 oral / speaking, 3 revise, 4 written, 5 pass, 6 essay, 7 retake, 8 true or false, 9 practical, 10 do, 11 multiple-choice, 12 fail, 13 cheat

c 2 practical, 3 written, 4 revised, 5 oral / speaking, 6 passed, 7 retook, 8 cheat, 9 did, 10 true or false, 11 multiple-choice, 12 essays, 13 failed

## 2 PRONUNCIATION

a /eɪ/ essay, fail, retake
/æ/ campus, exam, practical
/ɑː/ marks, pass, seminar
/ə/ oral, similar

c 2 cheat, 3 could, 4 written, 5 report, 6 guess, 7 multiple, 8 true, 9 revise, 10 choice

## 3 GRAMMAR

a 2 I've known, 3 was shining, 4 is giving out, 5 she's going to, 6 I had, 7 I took, 8 He spoke, 9 I'll lend, 10 he'd spent

b 2 to make, 3 am / 'm going, 4 were built, 5 have / 've, had, cut, 6 couldn't start, 7 would / 'd lose, 8 used to live, 9 doesn't / didn't love, 10 would / 'd have spoken

c 2 had / 'd already done
3 had / 'd been told
4 was driving
5 didn't say
6 stopped
7 had / 'd passed
8 couldn't
9 have / 've been driving
10 is / 's being repaired
11 would / 'd buy
12 have / 've just been offered
13 will / 'll be able to
14 am / 'm going to get
15 won't go

d Students' own answers

OXFORD
UNIVERSITY PRESS

Great Clarendon Street, Oxford, OX2 6DP, United Kingdom

Oxford University Press is a department of the University of Oxford. It furthers the University's objective of excellence in research, scholarship, and education by publishing worldwide. Oxford is a registered trade mark of Oxford University Press in the UK and in certain other countries



The moral rights of the author have been asserted

First published in 2020

2024 2023 2022 2021 2020

10 9 8 7 6 5 4 3 2 1



ISBN: 978 0 19 403920 8

Printed in China

This book is printed on paper from certified and well-managed sources

ACKNOWLEDGEMENTS

*Back cover photograph*: Oxford University Press building/David Fisher

The authors would like to thank all the teachers and students round the world whose feedback has helped us to shape English File.

*The authors would also like to thank*: all those at Oxford University Press (both in Oxford and around the world) and the design team who have contributed their skills and ideas to producing this course.

Finally very special thanks from Clive to Maria Angeles, Lucia, and Eric, and from Christina to Cristina, for all their support and encouragement. Christina would also like to thank her children Joaquin, Marco, and Krysia for their constant inspiration.

*The publisher would like to thank the following for their permission to reproduce photographs*: Alamy Stock Photo pp.12 (toothbrush/Danny Smythe), 26 (lid/Dudley Wood), 26 (pot/studiomode), 26 (cola/pumkinpie), 26 (jar/RTimages), 26 (tub/Lenscap), 26 (carton/Nikreates), 26 (bottle/incamerastock), 26 (packet/Carolyn Jenkins), 26 (wrapper/Chris Haye), 26 (carrots/Dorling Kindersley ltd), 26 (box/B.A.E. Inc.), 26 (polystyrene tray/Metta digital), 26 (best before/David J. Green - food themes), 32 (weather report/Mark Richardson), 34 (The Poker House 2008/AF archive), 43 (sewing/lolostock), 45 (gluing/fStop Images GmbH), 55 (ponytail/Ellen Isaacs), 55 (haircut/Agencja Fotograficzna Caro), 55 (a parting/Emotive Images), 55 (fringe/LatinStock Collection), 55 (bunches/YAY Media AS), 58 (bomb damage/Trinity Mirror/Mirrorpix); Alonso Herranz Hudson p.21 (woman in garden); Getty Images pp.4 (Agatha Christie/Popperfoto), 28 (garage/UpperCut Images), 32 (emperor penguins/Sylvain Cordier/hemis.fr), 45 (tying shoelace/Brad Wilson), 45 (assembling furniture/monkeybusinessimages), 47 (delivering groceries/SolStock), 52 (chatting/gradyreese), 55 (wedding hair/Jutta Klee), 55 (buzz cut/PhotoAlto/Sigrid Olsson), 55 (hair curled/AAGAMIA); Oxford University Press pp.12 (towel/sergign), 17 (car/Avatar_023), 26 (baby food/MM Studios), 35 (tractor/Taina Sohlman), 35 (sheep/Chris Hepburn), 35 (cockerel/Hintau Aliaksei), 35 (cow/smereka), 36 (Yorkshire Dales/Paul White), 45 (DIY/Paul Bradbury), 45 (drilling/RG Images), 45 (mending/Cathy Blackie), 45 (sewing/djem), 45 (changing tyre/DreamPictures/Blend Images), 50 (panda/ex0rzist), 50 (woman in snow/DJTaylor), 56 (gym/wavebreakmedia), 68 (New York/upthebanner); Shutterstock pp.4 (Katy Perry/DFree), 4 (Robert Downey Jr./Ga Fullner), 4 (Brad Pitt/Kathy Hutchins), 6 (reading stories/Monkey Business Images), 6 (student/Monkey Business Images), 7 (wall/Abstractor), 8 (tired woman/Prostock-studio), 11 (t-shirts/Tom Wang), 12 (headphones/Pixel-Shot), 12 (scissors/Kostenko Maxim), 12 (blank book/Dariusz Majgier), 12 (Stockholm/Adisa), 12 (battery/Oleksandr Kostiuchenko), 12 (washbag/Food Travel Stockforlife), 12 (First aid kit/Iasha), 12 (sunscreen/Jessica2), 12 (hairdryer/Nordling), 12 (beach bag/Anton Starikov), 12 (underwear/DN1988), 12 (razor/oksana2010), 15 (dirty bike/Oleksandr Berezko), 16 (bags/PoNing), 17 (sunflowers/Ivonne Wierink), 17 (watch/horiyan), 17 (sunscreen/Jessica2), 17 (notebook/FabrikaSimf), 17 (lamb chops/Robyn Mackenzie), 17 (tickets/Chinch), 17 (cupcakes/Ronald Sumners), 17 (closed sign/wedninth), 18 (baby/FamVeld), 18 (toddler/Gargonia), 18 (young girl/Monkey Business Images), 18 (boy/Tutti Frutti), 18 (teen boy/Monkey Business Images), 18 (young woman/Monkey Business Images), 18 (man/AJR_photo), 18 (woman/Dubova), 18 (senior couple/goodluz), 19 (hopscotch/Vladislav Gajic), 19 (listening/Antonio Guillem), 20 (grandmother & girl/Pressmaster), 23 (couple with cat/Minerva Studio), 23 (young boy/Olga Enger), 24 (couple/Syda Productions), 25 (taking pictures/ElRoi), 26 (tin/urbanbuzz), 26 (bottles/Teerasak Ladnongkhun), 27 (baby/Oksana Kuzmina), 28 (departure board/Eviart), 29 (University of Manchester/amirraizat), 30 (interview/Stokkete), 30 (money/Linda Bestwick), 31 (students/alfpoint), 35 (farm/Steve McDonald), 35 (barn/Annzee), 35 (donkey/Helga Madajova), 35 (lambs/Lukas Gojda), 35 (chickens/Elena Larina), 36 (cycling/Halfpoint), 37 (runners/CandyBox Images), 38 (travellers/Arts Illustrated Studios), 39 (farmer/Torwaistudio), 40 (mug/unatictm), 40 (oil & vinegar/Mateusz Gzik), 40 (candles/Octavian 707), 40 (tea/Kichigin), 40 (dish/photographyfirm), 40 (cutlery/Donovan van Staden), 40 (napkin/dvoevnore), 40 (salt & pepper/kan_khampanya), 40 (espresso/navorolphotography), 40 (glass/Mr.younglek), 42 (cafe/CandyBox Images), 45 (electrician/Andrey_Popov), 45 (cake maker/Ermolaev Alexander), 46 (ATM/cozyta), 48 (Bristol/Sion Hannuna), 48 (bedtime/yda Productions), 49 (stage/Kozlik), 51 (football match/Alfonso de Tomas), 53 (band/Freedom Studio), 54 (straighteners/The Dragonfly), 54 (dentist/Serhii Bobyk), 54 (plumber/Africa Studio), 54 (washing car/Photographee.eu), 54 (office worker/fizkes), 54 (hair cut/alexkich), 54 (DIY/Gorgev), 54 (cold woman/stockfour), 55 (highlights/frantic00), 55 (perm/schankz), 55 (straightening/MilanMarkovic78), 55 (hair wash/DenisProduction.com), 55 (blow-dry/ESB Professional), 55 (hair dyeing/DenisProduction.com), 55 (plaits/BestPhotoStudio), 55 (bleached hair/Kiselev Andrey Valerevich), 55 (shave/Corepics VOF), 56 (gym/Monkey Business Images), 56 (weightlifting/Flamingo Images), 56 (sit-ups/Stephen McCluskey), 56 (press ups/Aliona Hradovskaya), 56 (treadmills/bluedog studio), 56 (gyms/Dreams Come True), 56 (aerobics/Syda Productions), 56 (pilates/Andrey_Popov), 56 (stretching/djile), 56 (exercise bikes/Lucky Business), 56 (yoga/Gyorgy Barna), 57 (bride & groom/Myronovych), 57 (Blenheim Palace/Hendra Oktavianus), 58 (bow/wk1003mike), 58 (arrow/Andrey Burmakin), 58 (archer/vadimmmus), 58 (helmet/Sibrikov Valery), 58 (shield/Andrey_Kuzmin), 59 (Salisbury cathedral/Heiko Kalweit), 59 (Edinburgh Castle/Philip Birtwistle), 59 (Blackpool tower/Pefkos), 59 (Whitby Abbey/Gail Johnson), 59 (Kensington Palace/irisphoto1), 61 (hug/Mr.Whiskey), 61 (party/Halfpoint), 62 (conference/SmartPhotoLab), 62 (annoyed woman/ESB Professional), 63 (wedding rings/bondvit), 64 (boy & girl/Myroslava Malovana), 65 (wedding/Monkey Business Images), 65 (woman on phone/VGstockstudio), 67 (wedding cake/Leon Rafael), 70 (Elisabeth Moss/DFree), 71 (lab students/Lordn), 71 (cheating/awpixel.com), 73 (reception desk/Mangostar), 73 (driving test/michaeljung); Shutterstock Editorial pp.4 (Sting/Kamil Piklikiewicz), 4 (Bruno Mars/Jim Smeal/BEI), 4 (Ruth Rendell/ITV), 32 (Coronation Street/ITV), 32 (Gordon and Matilda Ramsay/Ken McKay/ITV), 32 (House of Commons/Gavin Rodgers), 32 (The Simpsons Movie 2007/Moviestore), 32 (The Crown TV Series 2016/Netflix/Kobal), 49 (basketball/Matt Slocum/AP).

*Illustrations by*: John Haslam p.60; Victor McLindon/Advocate Art p.70; Roger Penwill p.22.